Body and Mind
in Zulu Medicine

STUDIES IN ANTHROPOLOGY

Under the Consulting Editorship of E. A. HAMMEL,
University of California, Berkeley

Body and Mind
in Zulu Medicine

An Ethnography of health and disease in
Nyuswa–Zulu thought and practice

HARRIET NGUBANE
University of Edinburgh

1977

ACADEMIC PRESS
LONDON   NEW YORK   SAN FRANCISCO
A Subsidiary of Harcourt Brace Jovanovich, Publishers

Academic Press Inc. (London) Ltd
24–28 Oval Road
London NW1

US edition published by
Academic Press Inc.
111 Fifth Avenue,
New York, New York 10003

Library of Congress Catalog Card Number: 76–16982
ISBN: 0–12–518250–3

Text set in 11/13 pt Monotype Baskerville, printed by letterpress,
and bound in Great Britain at The Pitman Press, Bath

To the memory of my mother,

ANNASTASIA MAGUMEDE

Foreword

Dr Ngubane's monograph is a notable contribution to a branch of anthropological research that is rapidly expanding on both sides of the Atlantic. The anthropology of health and disease is concerned with what are surely the most vital and insistent preoccupations of all mankind, preoccupations that no miracles of scientific medicine will ever wholly abolish. What anthropological research is bringing to light is that, universal as these preoccupations are, there are striking differences in the ways different human communities evaluate and explain health and confront disease. Does this then mean that there is nothing common to all mankind or to any major division of mankind in the ways they think about and manage problems of health and disease? The answer lies far ahead as yet. The important task, for the time being, is to accumulate detailed studies in particular communities, testing generalizations as we go along. Dr Ngubane's monograph is a work in this category. Its distinction lies in the combination of personal experience, as a member of the community with field research in the development of her inquiry, and in the availability of a large and splendid literature on the Zulu upon which she has drawn for amplification of her material.

The Zulu people have an almost legendary place in the history and in the national consciousness of their native South Africa, among their Bantu as well as among their white fellow-countrymen. Their rise to power and hegemony, 150 years ago, under the leadership of Shaka, the military and political genius who has been called the

"Black Napoleon" (see Reader, 1966) and his successors is a frequent topic of literary and historical writing and is also deeply embedded in the folk memories of both black and white South Africans. The devasting inter-tribal wars and migrations and the clash with the Boer Trekkers that ended with the Battle of the Blood River in 1838 (since commemorated in the annual public holiday of Dingaan's Day on December 16th) left indelible marks on the course of South African history. It is of interest to find that the word "Zulu", according to the O.E.D., was in use as early as 1824 to refer to "a warlike race of South African Blacks". But the image of the Zulu as a proud, fierce, recklessly brave though barbaric warrior race was probably most vividly stamped on the popular imagination in Britain by the disaster of Isandlwana and the defence of Rorke's Drift in the "Zulu War" of 1879–80. The eventual defeat of the Zulus, the annexation of their country to Natal, the suppression of the rebellion of 1906 that was precipitated by the resented poll tax, the consequent abolition of the Zulu kingship and the dissolution of the nation into its constituent tribal units, put an end to their war-making powers and military organization. Today, of course, they live scattered in tribal locations and in urban and industrial areas, enmeshed in the modern industrial economy and separatist political constitution of the Republic like all the other Bantu peoples of South Africa. Christianity and literacy, modern commercial and technical occupations, Western values and forms of knowledge, and some of the professions based on higher education, are all part of Zulu social life. But this has not meant abandonment of all traditional ideas and values. In particular, it has not destroyed the basic patterns of Zulu family structure and neighbourhood relations.

As I have already indicated, Zulu ethnography and social history is exceptionally well documented. Travellers, traders, government officials and above all such missionary scholars as Callaway and Bryant have been adding to this literature for 150 years. More recently, especially since Professor Eileen Krige's classical survey of the literature 40 years ago (see reference in Dr Ngubane's bibliography) the corpus has been greatly expanded by the researches of professional anthropologists, linguists and other specialists, among them several Zulu scholars. And, as I have remarked, Dr Ngubane draws frequently on this literature to amplify, confirm or check on her own observations. The significant point about this is that, as regards the descriptive facts of custom, social organization, modes of thought and the general institutional framework, Nyuswa society is not substantially different today from what the rural Zulu were like forty or fifty years ago. There is direct evidence for this in the monograph by the distinguished Zulu anthropologist Professor A. Vilakazi (listed in Dr Ngubane's bibliography).

There is, therefore, little that is new in the descriptive data Dr Ngubane adduces. What is new and illuminating is her analysis and interpretation of the data. Writing as a professional anthropologist she works steadily within the framework of modern theory. But to this she adds insight that comes from her vantage point as a member of the society she is describing and this makes all the difference.

Her central topic is how the Nyuswa perceive and cope, conceptually and practically, with the problems of health and disease as these present themselves in their normal experience. Taking the reader step by step, with elegant clarity and lucidity, through her analysis, she unfolds a system of ideas, beliefs and practices that cannot fail to impress the reader with its subtlety and profundity. To begin with we are introduced to Zulu notions of health as the outcome of a balance in the relationship of man to environment, which is thought of not merely as the geographical and ecological background to social life but as ambience of individual and family life charged with mystical forces and hazards. Within this environment one is safe; danger comes from the outside. Disease represents a disturbance of the balance, so treatment is directed to restoring it.

What then are the possible causes of a disturbance of the health balance? Pursuing this question takes Dr Ngubane to what I consider to be the heart of her inquiry. In classical anthropological style, she examines a problem of wide generality in the mirror of a single society's modes of thought. Ethnographers have previously reported that among the Zulu certain forms of illness are attributed to sorcery, that some afflictions are associated with the ritual pollution that is believed to follow childbirth and contact with death, that black, red and white medicines have different applications, and so forth. What we have hitherto lacked is an analysis of the kind presented by Dr Ngubane in which these ideas and beliefs are related to the contexts of family life and social organization in which they emerge. When this is done it appears that the most dangerous form of sorcery according to Zulu belief is that which can only be imputed to a male family head, and that this occurs in situations of family tension that arise from the cleavages in family structure. Thus beliefs in sorcery far from being reducible to primitive superstition are understandable as customary devices for bringing into the open stresses and conflicts intrinsic to the family system and so making it possible to cope with them.

The family system is at the centre of the whole, elaborate scheme of ideas, beliefs and practices relating to health and disease. It is typically patrilineal and patriarchal, which means that women are always legally subordinate to men as the daughters and sisters of fathers and brothers or as the wives and mothers of husbands and sons. But whereas daughters and sisters are expendable, in the sense that they must be married out, wives and mothers are indispensable in order to fulfil every man's supreme hope of being able to leave male offspring. Thus it is that the most critical family tensions arise in relation to rights over the reproductive powers of women; and, *per contra*, it is by virtue of their socially and psychologically indispensable roles as wives and mothers that women obtain redress for their legal inferiority, in the shape of specialized but socially indispensable ritual roles; and this, Dr Ngubane shows is the key to the significance of pollution concepts and taboos in Zulu social life and to such apparent inconsistencies as the allocation to men of supremacy in the ancestor cult while the practice of divination, which is the medium of communication with the ancestors, is restricted to women and male transvestites.

Ritual symbolism plays a major part in resolving such contradictions and it is in her elucidations of the symbolic elements of the beliefs and practices she is examining that Dr Ngubane's unique understanding of Zulu culture comes especially to the fore. She gives special attention to the linguistic aspect, clarifying skillfully complexities that are apt to frustrate readers who do not know the language. In this connection she shows how Zulu ideas and beliefs about health and disease pre-suppose a conception of human nature and the human life cycle as part of a totality that can best be designated as the cosmos. Without this background the characteristic Zulu procedures in the treatment of illness and in prophylactic medication cannot be understood. Her analysis of the significance of emetics for the physical and spiritual cleansing that is basic to Zulu medication shows up cogently the rationale behind their notions of contagion and of mystical affliction. This is related to what is to my mind an outstanding contribution to current theoretical discussion in social anthropology. I refer to her analysis of the normal sequence of black, red and white medicines in every course of treatment. We can see how it makes good symbolic sense for such a course to begin with the black medicine for the purging of the internal evil that is the cause of the malady, to go on to the red medicine as an intermediate step and to end with the white medicine as the emetic that restores purity and balance.

There is of course much more to this colour symbolism than I can discuss here, particularly in connection with the animal sacrifices that accompany medication. But I must content myself with a last example of Dr Ngubane's method.

It is a curious fact that in this patriarchal society the chief mourner at a funeral is a woman; and it is this woman who actually places the body in its burial niche in the well-known foetal position. How can this be explained? The answer, Dr Ngubane shows, lies in the role of woman as mother. At the beginning of the life cycle she delivers the individual into the world of the living; at the end, it devolves on her to deliver him symbolically into the other world, the world of the dead where he is, as it were, reborn as an ancestor; and the congruence of these roles is symbolically expressed in the pollution that follows both giving birth and contact with death.

This brings me back to Dr Ngubane's analysis of the position of women, or rather of womanhood in Zulu society. As her inquiry progresses it becomes increasingly apparent that it is the woman as mother, not the patriarchal, former warrior father who is at the centre of the family drama. The well-being of offspring depends primarily on her moral conduct, and the conflicts that provoke ancestral wrath and so give rise to affliction and illness are more likely to be due to discord between men over the lawful control of her fecundity than to economic or plain power struggles between them. The bearing of these observations on the general question of the status of women in a "male dominated" society is obvious.

I have said enough, I hope, to persuade the reader of the importance and the absorbing interest of Dr Ngubane's book. Let me conclude by noting that modern scientific medicine is also available to the Nyuswa. They have access to a hospital and to Western-trained doctors, and they make use of these facilities for many types of illness. But the traditional ways of interpreting and of coping with disease still maintain their hold, either for disease or affliction that is defined as peculiarly African or to fall back upon when Western medicine fails. Dr Ngubane rounds off her study with some reflections on the relations between the two systems and on the changes in the traditional ways that are increasingly apparent.

August, 1976   MEYER FORTES
King's College,
Cambridge

Acknowledgements

I am deeply indebted to the Ioma Evans-Pritchard Fellowship and the Philip Bagby Studentship, both of which afforded me the opportunity to revise my PhD thesis for publication. Also I am grateful to St Anne's College, Oxford, for their financial assistance with the typing of the revised version.

My thanks are due to various trusts which enabled me to undertake research and write up my PhD dissertation. The initial fieldwork was made possible by a Nuffield Foundation grant. The Ernest Oppenheimer Memorial Trust and the Esperanza Trust of The Royal Anthropological Institute of Great Britain and Ireland supported me throughout my period of study at Cambridge. The Ling Roth Research Fund and the Smuts Memorial Fund both enabled me to return to South Africa from Cambridge in order to engage in a further period of research. The Radcliffe-Brown Memorial Fund helped me with typing and binding expenses of the dissertation.

My thanks are extended to all those who helped in various ways to enable me to travel to England in the first place. These are Archbishop D. Hurley of Durban, Mr D. Grice of the Institute of Race Relations in Durban, Mr F. W. Knowles of Pinetown and Patricia de Trafford of London.

To my first teacher, Professor Eileen J. Krige, formerly of the University of Natal, I owe a great deal of gratitude. It was through her encouragement and inspiration that I decided to take up anthropology.

I am grateful also to the staff of the Department of Social Anthropology and the Institute for Social Research, both of the University of Natal, and especially to Professors J. Argyle and H. Watts, for assistance I received during my second period of research.

To Professor Sir Edmund Leach, Provost of King's College, Cambridge, I owe a special debt of gratitude.

To Professor Meyer Fortes I owe a debt of a personal nature. It was through his untiring encouragement that I was enabled to study in Cambridge. But, above all, what I particularly want to point out is this: in the South African situation, the inequality between races develops, in subtle ways, uncertainties and feelings of inadequacy among those who are underprivileged. Professor Fortes as my teacher and friend reassured me in a manner that created self-confidence and liberated me intellectually.

I am likewise thankful to those others who helped me in various ways at Cambridge and Oxford, particularly my colleagues in Social Anthropology, and my friends at St. Anne's College, Oxford, and at Lucy Cavendish College, Cambridge.

I am particularly grateful to the Nyuswa-Zulu people without whose cooperation I could never have written this book. Special mention is due to Mr and Mrs Richard Mdluli, who extended hospitality to me throughout my stay in the Nyuswa area.

Last, but not least, I thank my family, who had to put up with the inconveniences caused by my absence while I was working on the manuscript for this book.

I have previously published under my married name of Sibisi, but have decided to use my maiden name for professional purposes henceforth. This is also in accordance with Zulu custom whereby a woman does not change her surname on marriage.

August 1976   HARRIET NGUBANE

Contents

Introduction

Period of field work

I first went into the Nyuswa Reserve in August 1963 as a research student of Natal University. I lived as a guest of Mr and Mrs Richard Mdluli for a continuous period of seven months. After that I visited the Reserve intermittently. I also maintained contact through some Nyuswa migrants who worked in my home town (Pinetown), about 20 to 25 miles away from the Nyuswa area. In addition I spent three months among the Ximba-Zulu of Umkhambathini, a chiefdom in the Valley of a Thousand Hills. This I did in order to assess the differences between the Nyuswa and the Ximba—and I concluded that the basic notions I found among the former also obtained among the latter. In 1971 I returned to South Africa from Cambridge and engaged in eight months' further research among the Nyuswa people. Between 1958 and my own field work in 1963, I had worked intermittently as a research assistant with Professor Eileen Krige of the University of Natal (Krige, 1967). This introduced me not only to research techniques and a wide range of rituals, but also took me to different parts of Kwa-Zulu—an experience that has enabled me to examine in this book the basic tenets of Zulu cosmology.

Choice of people

The Nyuswa–Zulu had already been studied by two Zulu social anthropologists: Dr A. Vilakazi (1962) and Mr M. B. Mbatha (1960).

These studies gave me a background knowledge of Nyuswa social organization. They also meant that the Nyuswa people were already acquainted with social anthropologists. This was an advantage. But I was very much aware that there was another side to it which could be disadvantageous. This caused me to keep in mind that the people's patience and tolerance could be tried to breaking point by the intrusion of outsiders into their lives, and that being expected to answer incessant questions could irritate them.

Choice of subject

Both Vilakazi and Mbatha in their studies of the Nyuswa people were mainly concerned with the dynamics of change.

My own choice of subject was influenced by a desire to look into social behaviour that was considered traditional and was referred to by the people themselves as "doing things in a Zulu way" (*Sigcina isiZulu*). This suggests that the people see Zulu institutions as a heritage worth preserving and defending against intrusive ideas or conflicts arising from new or alien contacts.

Since a study of this nature brings out some fundamental framework of the world view within which social interaction takes place, I was keen to attempt preserving it in writing more particularly because in these days of social mobility and rapid change the Zulu philosophy of life could be lost to posterity. Such a study could further provide a basis for understanding change in the field of cosmology, health and disease. A good knowledge of what people change from is a prerequisite for understanding directions in transformations.

Personal background

I am Zulu. I was born of Catholic parents and was brought up within an almost homogeneously Catholic community which surrounded a Catholic mission station. I received all my education prior to university at Catholic schools. I was trained as a teacher and I have always taught in Catholic schools.

Catholicism seeks to change those areas of Zulu culture and social life which most obviously conflict with the moral rules and religious teaching of the Church. This means that in certain aspects such as the recognition of ancestral power, the consulting of a diviner (*isangoma*) and polygamous or levirate marriage, the Church seeks change. But other aspects of traditional social life are sustained. Examples of this are marriage exchanges (*lobolo*), kinship patterns, and the consultation of doctors (*izinyanga*).

So I was raised in a community which presented only part of traditional Zulu culture, thereby leaving gaps in my knowledge and experience.

The community I grew up in was large, with a cross-section of old and young people, literate and illiterate; some of these people were very poor and others relatively well off. When I married I lived for almost twenty years in a much smaller community, made up of professional people who were mainly teachers at one of the largest African Catholic boarding schools in the country. Families were without their elderly relatives.

The relevance of this to my background experience is that I was cut off from a larger community at a time when I had just attained a status of "adulthood", for it is the married people, because of the responsibility they are now expected to undertake, who acquire from their seniors a deeper insight into their culture. A married woman usually acquires such knowledge from her mother-in-law.

Disadvantages

When in 1963 I went to live in Nyuswa territory, my background proved to be a handicap in many ways. At the beginning I made a number of blunders which would have been more tolerable in a non-Zulu person. I will give one instance to illustrate this point.

In a certain Christian home there were several goat skins used to cover the floor in the living room. I later found that in another room there was a second pile of goat skins. I told the woman of the house that I would like to buy a few of the skins if they could spare them for sale. In reply she asked what had happened to my goat skins. When I told her that we never had any, because we never slaughtered goats, she looked bewildered and said that I was joking, as no Zulu could survive without occasionally sacrificing to the ancestors. When her husband arrived later in the day, she told him of my request. He also wanted to know what had happened to the skins of the goats we slaughtered. At that point I became uneasy and realized that it could be disastrous if I

insisted on telling the truth. So I prevaricated. I said that although we
slaughtered occasionally my husband was careless with the skins. He
left them outside and they were usually destroyed by dogs. This answer
brought relief to both. The man advised me to take care of the
skins myself in future. I was later to learn that whereas skins of oxen
slaughtered for sacrifice were readily sold, sacrificial goat skins were
considered to have certain "sacred" properties and their right place was
in the home. If, for instance, in sacrifice an ox and a goat are killed,
the goat always precedes the ox by a day, and this has a special ritual
significance.

The importance of this anecdote is that it illustrates how my accepta-
bility differed from that of a non-Zulu anthropologist. People in the
traditional setting would find it difficult to believe that I was a Zulu
and yet did not regard ancestors as important in my life. Usually a
Christian Zulu living in a chiefdom does not find Christian beliefs and
ancestral beliefs incompatible. These two beliefs exist side by side,
perhaps because there are fewer pressures to renounce the ancestors in
a community not homogeneously Christian. My task was to convince
the people that although I was an educated Zulu, I did not look down
upon Zulu tradition. I told them that I had the disadvantages of my
mission background which denied me proper insight into Zulu culture.
I also pointed out that my presence among them was motivated by the
desire to fill in the gaps in my knowledge.

My hostess, who was a teacher by training, soon realized my
problems. She proceeded in earnest to instruct me in the finer points
of Zulu etiquette (e.g. the protocol in the chiefly court).

Although my background was a handicap, certain advantages were
derived from it. I was in a position of "belonging and not belonging".
One result was that I could not help being struck by certain rituals and
practices which I would otherwise have taken for granted. For instance,
one of the things that struck me forcefully was the role of a diviner and
her position in the community. She was the opposite of the image I had
had of her. As we shall see later, I found that she held a leading position
in the community and commanded respect and confidence because of
high moral standards which her position demanded of her.

Many Zulu ceremonies and rituals would have been part of my
upbringing had I been a non-Christian Zulu. Yet I might have been
involved emotionally in ways that could have hindered my interpretation and objectivity.

Advantages

In most aspects of daily life, outlook and habits, I am Zulu in spite of my mission background. Above all, Zulu is my mother tongue. This meant not only that I could carry out my research without assistants (except for a short period when I was collecting quantitative data on family composition and was assisted by a local ex-teacher), but that I could establish immediate rapport with informants of all social levels.

My host traced connection with my mother's clan, while his wife traced connection with my own clan (*isibongo*). In this sense I was a cousin (*umzala*) to them both and I was treated as one of the family.

Living as part of the family allowed me to participate in the family gatherings in the evenings and to share the local gossip. In this way I was introduced into the intimate social relations of the community. In addition, my hostess happened to be a dental specialist, whose patients most often came during the night, desperate for pain-relieving treatment which she often successfully gave. Her knowledge was a family prerogative which had been passed down for generations. I had the opportunity of watching her at work.

Being black was one of the greatest advantages I had, for in the South African setting a white anthropologist is associated through colour with other white people whose relationship with the African people is that of master and servant.

The question that arises is whether I could have managed to write up material of this nature as an educated Zulu without any training in social anthropology.

I do not think it would have been possible.

My training enabled me to see beyond my personal experience as a Zulu.

Reading other studies gave me a comparative frame that served to focus upon distinctive features of social organization which experience derived only from my personal knowledge of my society would not have revealed.

My awareness of the possible influence of patterns of social structure and of ideological frames of reference and the kinds of problems which other studies have shown enabled me to look at my society more detachedly and to recognize distinctive qualities of Zulu forms.

Because most able-bodied men were away in the town centres, I spent most of my time talking to women. This suited me well, since I had a lot in common with my respondents. However, I soon realized that there

were certain issues which required further clarification. One illustration of this was in connection with the activities of the ancestors. Some
women informants blamed their illness and misfortune on the capricious
nature of female spirits. It became apparent that the ancestors thus
blamed were usually mothers-in-law, against whom the accuser had no
supporting evidence such as that of a diviner or of a general family con-
census. Very often the husband had a different version from the wife,
which she did not dispute in his presence, but refuted privately to me.
It did not take much probing to discover that there had been an
ambivalent relationship between wife and mother-in-law during the
latter's lifetime, which was extended by the former and projected into
the spirit world. What I learnt from this was the relevance of "who the
respondent is" in an interview. To minimize any bias personal factors
of this nature might introduce, I tried to strike a balance by checking particular items of information against more general rules; and I was thus in
a position to discriminate between the exceptions and the general rules.
As an illustration of this I have appended some texts (pp. 159–166)
which exemplify the basic information in which I found no contradictory evidence and on which I base most of my analysis and conclusions.

Method

During my first stay in the Nyuswa area I spent most of my time in
getting to know the people. In the process I learnt much about what
constitutes good or ill-health from the Nyuswa point of view.

When in 1969 I went to Cambridge I tried to make use of the data I
had collected. I realized that there were many questions that I could
not answer. Having isolated areas in my data which needed further
research or verification, I returned to the Nyuswa Reserve in 1971.

I want to stress that the opportunity of returning to do more field
work, after having tried to analyse the data I had gathered during my
first period of research, was extremely useful. I began to ask new questions in a much more systematic and better structured manner. My
perception was sharpened and my inquiry was much more penetrating.
I had drawn up two questionnaires. One with open-ended questions
written in Zulu and English was intended as a guide to explore indigenous notions of health (I was influenced by the notion of "aide-
memoire" in Firth *et al.*, 1970). With the other schedule I sought
quantitative data from a hundred homesteads, about family composition, marriage, illness and death. These data enabled me in certain

areas to check my theoretical hypotheses against the realities. This has been useful, for example, in determining the frequency of various types of causation to which death and illness are attributed as will be seen in Chapter 7.

My inquiry was not confined to the Nyuswa chiefdom. I visited out-patient sections of the nearest hospital, clinics and private surgeries, all of which drew patients from the various parts of the valley, with a view to contacting patients and discussing their ailments. I was interested in why they had chosen to come to that particular doctor or clinic, why they preferred Western types of treatment, what other treatments they had undertaken or tried before, and what they really thought was the matter with them.

I was also able to discuss casually Zulu notions that I regarded as basic to Zulu cosmology or of which I had received conflicting interpre-tations. I used to ask questions or make statements which provoked debates in a bus, in a train, at the bus rank or anywhere where people were likely to discuss such matters and express their views. This may sound unusual to the English reader, but it must be understood that Zulu find nothing wrong in entering into conversation with an African stranger. I found these exchanges extremely stimulating and rewarding. Often they not only confirmed information I had collected within Nyuswa territory but they brought additional enlightenment on various issues. For this reason I am confident that what I have written in the following chapters represents a common basis of Zulu notions which form central tenets of outlook.

Since I wanted to be as inconspicuous as possible I used field work equipment such as cameras and tape-recorders as little as possible, since these are symbols of affluence and much more identified with white anthropologists, and therefore outsiders, in apartheid South Africa. For the same reason I also avoided recording material in public. In public ceremonies I often joined in the songs and learnt them by heart in order to write them down afterwards. Whereas in private interviews it was much easier to make written notes as a person spoke, in casual and group interviews people tended to become tense and formal if they realized that what they said was being written down.

In writing up this material I have had to cope with a problem of translating, not only because English is not my native language, but also because there are various Zulu concepts that are not easily trans-latable. For instance, I translate *umuzi* as "homestead" even though

I know that these two words do not really mean the same thing, but it is the closest English term I can get. The same applies to "pollution", "sacrifice", "marriage" and various other terms which in Zulu do not express the same notion as the English terms. Here is one illustration. "Marriage" in Zulu is *ukwenda* (lit. travel a long journey). To a Zulu this term conjures up the rituals which are calculated to integrate the bride into her husband's family. It is thus the woman who is "married" into her husband's family, rather than the union of a man and wife at marriage as in the English sense. It is about niceties of this nature which get lost in translation that I want to warn the reader.

I have also had to cope with another and different kind of translation problem. Since I belong to the society which is the subject of anthropological study, I am aware of the feelings and suspicions of the people studied, regarding anthropological terminology. For this reason I have replaced terms in common use with anthropological terms, such as "kraal" with "homestead"; "magic" with "ritual"; "symbolism" or "religion"; "tribe" with "chiefdom"; "medicine-man" with "doctor"; "witchdoctor" with "diviner".

The problem of terminology is a complex one. I do not claim to have solved it, as there are various ambiguous words which cause a great deal of confusion. For instance, the Zulu use the term *inkosi* to refer to a king, a chief and God. They also use one term *uzalo* or *umndeni* to refer to all levels of lineage units. Since English terminologically distinguishes between these various categories, translation from Zulu to English often becomes ambiguous.

The contribution

Some of the ethnographic material which I bring out in this work has not previously appeared in anthropological literature. There is, however, a considerable amount which I have drawn from published sources. With regard to such material my field researches have enabled me to note and to bring out or highlight new facets relevant to my subject.

However, the main virtue of this study lies, I believe, in that it does not only attempt to present Zulu thought and practice regarding health and disease within the framework of Zulu cosmology, seen as an integrated whole. It also reveals the nature of opposition between the sexes in a patrilineal society which practises rigid exogamous rules.

1 | The People and Their Land

Historical background

The Nyuswa Reserve lies within what is popularly known as the "Valley of a Thousand Hills" in Natal, South Africa. This is about 35 miles on the north-western side of Durban.

The genealogy of the Nyuswa royal family (see Fig. 1) maintains that Nyuswa was a grandson of a man called Ngcobo. The surname or clan name (*isibongo*) of the Nyuswa people is therefore Ngcobo, though as members of a chiefdom they call themselves Nyuswa.

According to Nyuswa informants, about a hundred and thirty years ago their chief Ncume and his people settled in the present Nyuswa area, which was then unoccupied.

According to Bryant (1929, pp. 481–483), the Nyuswa since Senzan-gakhona's days (i.e. before King Shaka, at the turn of the 19th century), were situated in the northern parts of the Tugela Valley, near the Emamba stream which enters the Tugela river, about 30 miles from its mouth. They trace their descent (see Fig. 1) back to Vumezita, who had only two sons, Ngcobo and Mkeshane. The latter, because of his roving tendencies, was later named "Shangase" by his brother Ngcobo. The two brothers founded clan names known respectively as Ngcobo and Shangase.[1] Ngcobo had only one son, Dingila, who begot Nyuswa by the chief wife (*indlunkulu*). By the third wife (*iqadi*) he begot

---

[1] It is of interest to note that these two now occupy adjacent territories in the Valley of a Thousand Hills, belong to two separate chiefdoms, and even intermarry.

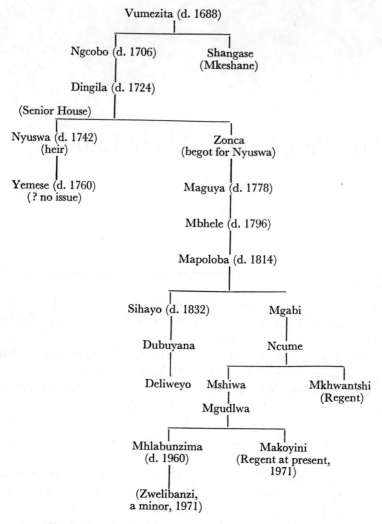

Fig. 1. Genealogy of the Nyuswa (From Bryant, 1929, p. 482.)

Ngotoma, whose descendants were later known as Amaqadi. They are today the Qadi chiefdom, which occupies a territory adjacent to Nyuswa. The descendants of Nyuswa were known as AmaNyuswa.

Nyuswa's son Yemese had no issue, so one of Nyuswa's brothers Zonca raised up seed for him, according to the Zulu custom of "raising a house" (*ukuvusa indlu*, discussed below in Chapter 4). The son born of this union was Maguya, who begot Mbhele, who begot Mapoloba.

Mapoloba was an old man when Shaka began to rule the Zulu. Mapoloba's chief wife bore him an heir, Miswayo. Soon after, Mapoloba died and so did the infant heir. So the Nyuswa people were left without a chief. However, Mapoloba left two influential sons, Sihayo and Mgabi, The latter, though ambitious, had fewer followers. In view of his insecure position, he planned to have Sihayo killed. He suggested a clan meeting to discuss the problem of succession. He had arranged with his partisans that during the course of the meeting Sihayo would be speared to death. Luckily for Sihayo the spear was caught in his shield. A fight then ensued between Mgabi's and Sihayo's followers.

When King Shaka heard of the incident he summoned both factions to appear before him and stood them in single file. To everyone's surprise he led his dog along the line. It sniffed at everybody, and when it came to Sihayo it lay down and wagged its tail. Shaka therefore declared Sihayo the rightful chief!

Such a choice, made by a mere dog, never satisfied Mgabi. He bided his time. After some years he developed new tactics by slandering Sihayo in such a way that King Shaka would spurn him. Sihayo used to send bundles of tobacco leaves to Shaka as a tribute. Mgabi spread rumours (making sure they reached the King's ears) that Sihayo had "doctored" the tobacco to harm the King's health.

Contrary to Mgabi's expectations, Shaka's army routed the whole Nyuswa clan, including Mgabi himself. But during the battle Sihayo was drowned in the Tugela river.[1] Much later, during the regime of Sir Theophilus Shepstone (after 1845), his followers were offered a settlement at the Noodsberg hills in Natal. There they still are, under a chief directly descended from Sihayo.

But the Nyuswa we are concerned with are the descendants of the Mgabi group. Of this group Bryant writes:

> In long after years, still rather disgruntled over their beating, the Mgabi-ites went off and bought themselves a farm southward of the Mzimkhulu, and there Mshiwa, son of Ncume, son of Mgabe, still reigns over a little kingdom of his own . . . while his brother, Mkwantshi, *busa's* [reigns] over a small Government patch near Camperdown.
>
> 1929, p. 483

It is the people of this "small Government patch near Camperdown" who concern us here.

[1] There may be some historical error here in that Bryant mentions 1832 as the year when Sihayo died, yet Shaka died in 1828.

According to Nyuswa informants, Ncume was the first Nyuswa chief to settle in the present Nyuswa area in the Valley of a Thousand Hills. His son Mshiwa was asked by Sir Theophilus Shepstone (who in 1845 became the Diplomatic Agent of Natives and in 1852 the Secretary of Native Affairs in Natal), to settle on land in the Harding district, the southern tip of Natal.

The statements of the Nyuswa tally with the account given by Morris. He writes:

> Shepstone's reserves varied in size, one of them ran to 400,000 acres. They were carefully chosen to interfere as little as possible with the existing cluster of farms. They separated traditionally hostile clans and they also served as buffers. Natives were packed into the vacancies to the South where they formed a belt between Natal and AmaMpondoland, . . . In all, Shepstone moved some 80,000 Natal Kaffirs about on the complicated ethnic chessboard of Natal, and only twice in three decades did he have to resort to force.
>
> 1966, p. 173

The Nyuswa are not mentioned specifically by Morris, but he suggests that Mshiwa must have been one of the chiefs sent to "form a belt between Natal and AmaMpondo".

When Chief Mshiwa went to Harding he left his brother Mkhwantshi behind to rule as regent. After his death no other regent was appointed. Instead, only the headmen (*izinduna*) nowadays represent the chief. The chiefly heir, Zwelibanzi, is a minor. His father's brother, Makoyini, who is the acting chief, comes periodically from Harding, more than a hundred miles away, to hear the headmen's reports and to decide difficult cases that are held over to await his judgement. He has a house in the area, which is looked after by a caretaker.

The Nyuswa Reserve straddles two magisterial districts, Pinetown and Camperdown. For this reason there are two headmen, one representing each district. They are a point of contact between the South African Government and the Nyuswa people.

For administrative purposes, such as trying cases or listening to important Government pronouncements through the Bantu Commissioners, the Nyuswa people gather together in the presence of both headmen. No case is tried in the absence of one, even if the litigants belong to a single magisterial district. In other words, while the Nyuswa people are divided at the level of the South African Government, they endeavour to be united at the level of chiefdom government.

Headmanship is not hereditary. A headman is appointed by the chief and approved by the people. In most cases he is a person who has previously held a lesser official position as, for instance, an assistant headman, and has proved capable. Alternatively, he may be a man who usually spoke intelligently at gatherings or at trials of cases, and thereby showed qualities of wisdom and leadership. He must be someone who can afford to stay at home, or work within the Reserve, to be available most of the time. If he later fails in his duties as a headman he can be deposed.

The chiefdom (*isizwe*), the clan (*isibongo*) and the lineage (*uzalo*)

A chiefdom is territorially defined.

It has already been pointed out that the term Nyuswa refers, most appropriately, to those who are descendants of Nyuswa himself and bear the surname (*isibongo*) Ngcobo.

The chief (*inkosi*) and most of the Nyuswa people belong to the Ngcobo clan. But not all descendants of the man, Nyuswa, still belong to the Nyuswa chiefdom. Some left the area and attached themselves to another chiefdom. This means that although still of the Ngcobo clan they are no longer Nyuswa "citizens". Within the Nyuswa itself, similarly, there are many people whose surname or clan name is not Ngcobo. But since they owe allegiance to the Nyuswa chief and are settled in his territory, they are now Nyuswa "citizens". In other words, although the Nyuswa chiefdom is essentially composed of the chief's clan, which is numerically dominant, it also contains people belonging to other clans. A man can change his chiefdom allegiance, but he cannot change his membership of a particular clan. All the chiefdoms collectively form the Zulu nation (*isizwe sakwaZulu*) and owe allegiance to the Zulu king (*inkosi*).[1]

Membership of a clan does not presuppose ties of consanguinity. A clan is exogamous; some clans observe certain clan marks and others have a clan anthem (*ihubo*). Yet others may have clan marks and an anthem.

Clans are divided into lineages. A lineage (*umndeni* or, much more commonly in Nyuswa, *uzalo*, from *zala*, to bear, hence "of common birth") is composed of people who can trace descent to a common agnatic ancestor. Lineage relationship presupposes ties of consanguinity through patrilineal descent.

A lineage is divided into segments. The members of each lineage

[1] This is mainly in theory as there is very little evidence of it in practice. Since Shepstone's days each chief has been directly responsible to the white government. The Zulu king is now referred to as Paramount Chief.

segment trace their descent to a common paternal grandfather.[1] This is the most important group within the lineage. Its members have mutual religious and social obligations; for instance, they may not practise sorcery (except "lineage" sorcery to be discussed later) against each other. If they quarrel, they must put things right by performing a special rite to appease the ancestors who sanction their behaviour. In addition, each segment has its leader and its own court which deals with lineage matters. Members of a segment usually occupy a contiguous area, generally referred to as the plain of the so-and-sos (*ukhalo lwakaNgcobo* or *lwakaNzama*—the plain of the Ngcobos or of the Nzamas). They distinguish themselves from other segments of the same lineage by referring to themselves as "the lineage members who eat together" (*siwuzalo oludla ndawonye*, i.e. the lineage members we sacrifice with). The other segments, such as those who share descent with them from a common great-grandfather but not grandfather, are referred to as "lineage members we no longer eat with" (*siwuzalo esingasadlelani nalo*, i.e. the lineage members we no longer share sacrifice with, which means that there are portions of sacrificial meat which are eaten only by this group and never given to the outsiders).

All the descendants of No. 1 in the kinship chart (Fig. 2) can be seen as constituting a lineage. But the fourth generation of descendants (i.e. the grandchildren of Nos 2, 3, 4, 5 and 6 who are homestead heads, *abanumzane*) constitute separate lineage segments. For instance, the lineage segment reflected on the chart is that which traces descent from No. 2, and has religious and jural obligations as a group distinct from segments founded by Nos 3, 4, 5 and 6. However, in the developmental cycle of the lineage segments there may be overlapping areas which are points of connection between one segment and the other. An example of this overlap is illustrated by Nos 17 and 18 on the chart. They are the only living members of their generation within the segment. In the other segments of the lineage there are still some living members of the same generation, and these together constitute a preceding lineage segment. In other words, Nos 17 and 18 on the chart belong to two lineage segments—that of their children's generations, and that of their own generation.

Zulu lineages are remarkably shallow in comparison with those of societies such as the Tallensi of Ghana (Fortes, 1949).

---

[1] See Fig. 2. This is a diagram of a real lineage segment and not a hypothetical one.

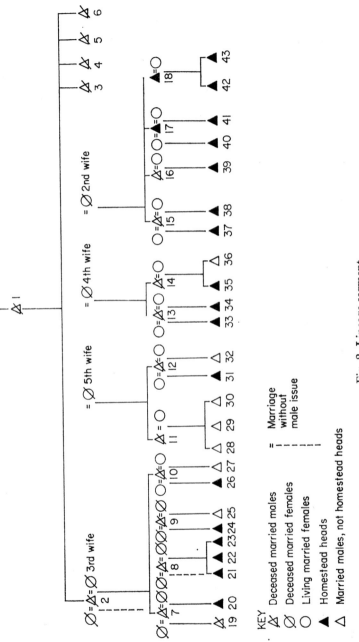

Fig. 2. Lineage segment.

Other recent students in the Zulu field have also noted the lack of depth of Zulu lineages. Thus Reader refers (1966, p. 80) to the "minimal descent group" (a term he chooses to use instead of lineage) as of three generations within which political or jural obligations as well as purely domestic and kinship ones can be held to apply.

Again, Vilakazi writes: "Very few commoners can go beyond their great-grandfathers in tracing their genealogies". (1962, p. 21.)

Mbatha (1960, p. 28) observes that even if the great-grandfather is known, people choose to recognize the descendants of their grandfather as the section of the lineage that matters.

Laredo, who did his research among the Zulu in the middle nineteen sixties, makes the same observation regarding the shallowness of lineages.[1]

These anthropologists agree with my own observations regarding the composition of the effective lineage segment.

The shallowness of lineage generational depth explains why people often fail to remember the names of their ancestors beyond the great-grandfather's generation. There is no pressing need to remember them, as they no longer belong to the effective group of ancestors. I also often found it difficult to get people to tell me the names of other descendants of their great-grandfather if such relatives had moved away from the territory. Yet they knew all the names of those who belonged to their own lineage segment, even if these had also left the area, since it is only within this group that jural and religious obligations operate. The chiefly families, however, are exceptions, in that they trace their genealogy many generations back; the obvious reason here is the importance of succession.

The difficulty facing a student of social anthropology is that in Zulu there is no terminology to distinguish between the effective lineage segment, i.e. descendants of a common grandfather, and the consanguineal ties which go beyond the grandfather. They are all referred to as *umndeni* or *uzalo* (of common birth), which is a term used in recognition of ties of consanguinity. The distinction is only made descriptively by reference to "those we eat with" and "those we no longer eat with" (i.e. we no longer sacrifice with).

The shallow span of jurally effective ancestors enables us to understand more clearly certain basic features related to health that will be discussed in later chapters.

[1] J. E. Laredo, University of Bradford. Personal communication.

Lineage membership is reckoned through homestead heads (*abanum-zane bemizi*). These are married men whose father and grandfather are deceased, and who form a link between the living and the dead by inter-ceding with the dead on behalf of their descendants. A homestead (*umuzi*) may be composed of a man, his wife (or wives) and children, at a particular point in time. Usually with the passage of time when the children grow up and the sons get married, there would be within the homestead a man, his wives, his sons and their wives, as well as their children. There may be in addition other relatives living within the homestead, such as the homestead head's unmarried sister or his widowed mother. The composition is never exactly the same, but usually each family becomes an extended family (i.e. more than one nuclear family) at some point because marriage is virilocal. Large extended families (*inxulmua*) usually segment after the death of the homestead head when the sons build their own independent homes on the lineage land.

Not all people belong to lineages within the Nyuswa reserve. Some homesteads which are relatively new in the area have no lineage links and depend for assistance in times of need on good neighbourliness, or on some other forms of relationship.

The landscape

The area shows two principal features. There is a relatively high plateau, referred to as *inkangala*, said once to have been fertile and to have produced tall and soft grass which was a delicacy to stock and was also used for thatching. This, however, has now given way to stunted and hard grass (*ingongoni*), which is said to be evidence of impoverished soil.

Adjoining either side of this plateau are steep hillsides ending in a low veld below, which is characterized by short thorny trees and shrubs that form a natural bush. This hilly, bushy and broken landscape is referred to as *ihlanze*. In former times it is said to have produced wild fruits and spinaches in abundance. These are now sparsely scattered. The natural bush provides firewood, carving poles and herbal medi-cines. It is well provided with water, as there are rivulets and water holes between the hills. The borders of these rivulets are highly valued for cultivation.

The Christianized younger families, and the newcomers, prefer the

inkangala (plateau) area. Consequently that area is more densely popu-
lated. Its attraction is further enhanced by the fact that the main shops,
the bus terminus, the biggest school, the dipping tanks, and the area
for court procedures are all in it.

Land tenure

The land is collectively owned by the Nyuswa chiefdom, with the chief
as principal executor and arbitrator in land affairs. No person can have
freehold rights to any piece of land. To have other land rights one must
be a Nyuswa "citizen". A person has a right over the land that he uses.
If he goes away to live in town, or allows the land to remain unused
over a long period, the land reverts to the chief, who may find better
use for it. In the chief's absence, matters of land distribution rest with
the two headmen.

Only male heads can be given building sites. An unmarried woman
cannot put up a house in her own right, neither can a widow. But if a
woman becomes widowed after having already built, no one can deprive
her of the land. Similarly, an unmarried girl can remain in her father's
home even if both parents have died. She cannot be evicted as long as
she continues to live there.

LAND HELD IN COMMON

There is common pasturage in the natural bush within the *ehlanzeni*
area. People can also collect dry wood and herbal medicines there, but
they may not cut down trees without first obtaining permission from
the headman.

Strips in between the fields, and fields that are not being cultivated
that season, can be used by anyone for grazing cattle. When the harvest
is over, all fields are open for grazing.

ALLOCATION OF LAND

An outsider seeking to settle within the Nyuswa area must have some-
body to vouch for him. This guarantor then becomes the host of the
newcomer and his family. He reports their presence in the area to the
headman. In the meantime, the neighbours observe and assess the new

family. After two or three months the host (with the newcomer) again approaches the headman from whom he requests permission to cut off a piece of land on his own holding for the newcomer. The headman appoints a day when he will "place" (*ukubeka*) the new man on the land. He also notifies the host's immediate neighbours, telling the homestead heads to come and witness this "placing" of a new family.

On the appointed day, the headman, neighbours, host and newcomer converge on the building site proposed. The headman invites objections and comments from the men present. The suitability of the building site is discussed. The fields are pointed out. Although no beacons are laid, natural signs are used to define the boundaries, for instance, rivers, hills, clusters of trees, or pathways. All the people present carefully note the boundaries, in case it becomes necessary to testify about them in some future dispute. Any men with objections or suggestions should voice them on this occasion, and not later. When there is general agreement, the newcomer gives R2.50 to the headman, who afterwards registers him at the Bantu Commissioner's Office. Henceforth he has all relevant rights to the land thus apportioned to him.

The lineage segment land is inherited by the heirs. But if segmentation of the extended family takes place, the "placing" of the lineage families follows the usual pattern described above. The headman and the lineage segment members are always present. On the lineage land, a man usually builds his home on the fields set aside for his wife's cultivation. Even then boundaries must be noted, as he may be given additional land. Any vacant and unused lineage segment land is under the charge of the segment head, who may distribute it among his dependents if there is need. He may not place any newcomer on that land without the permission of the segment members.

Newcomers are usually given land on the peripheries of lineage segment land, in such a manner that their homes are not interspersed among the lineage segment homesteads.

The area of land given to newcomers is much smaller than that held by the old residents. Those whose land is rather too small and unsuitable for cultivation can borrow strips from friends who have land to spare. This both helps the newcomer and puts into use land that would otherwise remain idle and thus liable to be claimed by the chief.

After paying the headman the sum of R2.50, a newcomer is not required to pay anything more for the use of land. He is, however, expected to observe certain duties for the benefit of the chiefdom. For instance, he should take an interest in its affairs, attend court cases and give his opinions.

A non-Zulu such as a Xhosa, Pondo, or Sotho, may be integrated into the chiefdom in this way. But people of non-African descent, such as Indians or English, cannot be, mainly because South African laws enforce separation of races.

The people

Vilakazi (1962) has emphasized the culture transformation that is taking place among the Nyuswa and Qadi. He cites Christianization as the main cause of the transformation. While this is true particularly in relation to observable material values reflected in type of house, furniture, and western dress, these Christians are nevertheless Zulu orientated, as they have been socialized more as Zulu than as English. I would argue that in spite of Christianity the permeating influence in the Nyuswa reserve is based more on Zulu culture than on any foreign culture. This is not only because a Zulu who wants to maintain his traditions and who believes only in his ancestral spirits lives side by side with Christians, but also because the values and the laws enforced by the chief's court are Zulu laws based on Zulu tradition and beliefs. For instance, if one is accused of sorcery, further confirmed by a diviner at a legal level, one is liable to be exiled and denied citizenship of the chiefdom, irrespective of whether one is an Anglican, a professional man, or a non-Christian. What I mean by "tradition" here is, of course, relative, as no society is static. I use the term for what the Nyuswa people themselves generally refer to as "the Zulu way of doing things" (ukugcina isizulu, to observe the Zulu culture).

Most people are illiterate, very few have gone beyond primary education, and fewer still are in professions such as teaching and nursing.

On the whole people are very poor, and therefore live on subsistence economy levels. Women till the fields, and most able-bodied men are in town either working or seeking work.

In the summer of 1971 a survey of 100 homesteads (1182 people)[1]

[1] There are no reliable population figures for the Nyuswa Reserve. Vilakazi (1961) gave an estimate of above 6,000. I would suggest that there may well be 10,000 people at present in view of the influx during the last decade arising from massive resettlement of the people in accordance with the policy of separate development.

showed that the following types of crops were planted (listed according to popularity): maize, beans, pumpkins, *amadumbe* (the Colocasia), sweet potato, peanuts, Bambarra groundnuts (*izindlubu*), sorghum (*amabele*), potatoes and sweet sorghum (*imfe*). The first four were planted by almost everyone. The new types of vegetables, such as cabbage, tomatoes, etc. require special care and water, and were therefore not widely planted. Only 18 homes had vegetable gardens. Of the western vegetables cabbage is the most popular, and is sold in local shops. Thirty homes had fruit trees, the commonest being peach trees. Agricultural yield is below subsistence level. There was no surplus in 1971 for storage or sale. Families depend much more on the wages earned by members working as migrant labourers.

Collectively, the homesteads surveyed possessed 352 cattle, 498 goats, 20 sheep, 60 pigs, 25 donkeys and several chickens. Donkeys are used as beasts of burden and also to pull the plough. They are not eaten. Pigs are bred for slaughter and the meat is sold locally. Goats are not milked. Chickens are not generally kept for egg-laying, but are bred for sale or for the pot. The sheep are a "Zulu type" which do not produce wool; they are reared for sale, feasts, or special rituals.

The following illustrates one important feature about the age range of the people dealt with in the survey (the figures are based on a sample of 1166).

	No.	%
Under 20 years	603	52
20–40 years	356	31
Over 40 years	207	17

These figures suggest that we are dealing with a group of people who are relatively young: less than half the population are more than 20 years' old, and roughly only one-sixth are more than 40. The inference is that on the whole Nyuswa have fairly short lives.

2 | Natural Causes of Illness

Before considering the different notions of what causes illness, I must point out that whereas in English the word "medicine" means substances that are used to restore health, the Zulu term *umuthi*, often used as a synonym for "medicine", has a wider connotation. *Umuthi* (pl. *imithi*) literally means "tree" or "shrub". When used for "medicine" it applies to noxious as well as curative substances. There is *umuthi wokwelapha*, medicine for healing, and *umuthi wokubulala*, medicine for killing. While some *imithi* are always used for healing and others for causing harm, still others can either heal or harm, depending on the motive for which they are used. It will be shown also in later chapters that some *imithi* are believed to be potent in themselves, and that no ritual or symbolic language is used in their administration, while others are symbolic and accompanied by special rites.

Another English term that requires attention is "disease". According to the Concise Oxford Dictionary the word "disease" means "a serious derangement of health, disordered state of an organism or an organ, any particular form of this with special symptoms and names". In Zulu the word *isifo* applies, as we shall see later, to disease that is manifested by somatic symptoms, to various forms of misfortune, and also to a state of vulnerability to misfortune and disease. In order to avoid confusion, I shall use the words "disease" and "medicine" in the Zulu sense.

In regarding nature as a factor in causation of illness, Zulu see natural forces as operating at two levels. The first is concerned with the body itself as a natural biological entity that presents somatic symptoms to indicate illness. The second is much more concerned with the role of ecological factors on health. I shall begin with the first level.

Illness as a biological factor

Most illnesses in this category are referred to generically as *umkhuhlane*. It is impossible to translate this very comprehensive term by any single expression in English. It refers mainly to illness that "just happens"— ranging from common colds to serious epidemics such as smallpox or influenza. Zulus believe that what is natural and alive has an inherent quality of breaking down of its own accord—it ages and dies. Besides the ageing process in general, certain bodily organs may break down individually, hence ulcers and decaying teeth. In addition, the malfunctioning of certain organs can disturb the whole body system and cause illness. For instance, excessive accumulation of the bile (*inyongo*) is said to cause headaches, biliousness and general debility.

Some diseases of this class are associated with stages in the growth of infants. Examples include measles, mumps (*uzagiga*), and physical irritation during teething.

Seasonal changes also bring about *umkhuhlane*. Outbreaks of diarrhoea (*uhudo*) and hay fever (*isithimulane*) are both associated with summer.

Susceptibility to certain types of disease is believed to run in certain families. These diseases include epilepsy (*isithuthwane*), chronic chest complaints such as asthma or chronic bronchitis (*ufuba*), and an unhealthy skin condition (*umzimba omubi*) marked by a tendency to develop sores, boils and other forms of skin complaints. Imbecility and strains of madness are also sometimes believed to run in families. Such diseases are referred to as *ufuzo* (resemblance).

None of the above-mentioned diseases results from any personal malice or a fault of the patient; they just happen. Although each has a specific name it can also be referred to as *umkhuhlane*, and I shall speak of them as a class unless there is a need to be specific.

The medicines used to cure diseases of the *umkhuhlane* class are believed to be potent and effective in themselves. They are therefore not ritualized. There is readiness to experiment, to try new medicines, or to discard some for better ones. There is also a general belief that the understanding of this type of natural illness is common to most people, including people from outside Africa. For this reason there is readiness to use curing techniques and medicine of Western type.

On the other hand, it is believed that non-Africans do not understand those notions of health and disease and causation of diseases, that are based on Zulu cosmology.

Diseases of this particular category are referred to as *ukufa kwabantu* "disease of the African peoples". The name is used mainly because the philosophy of causality is based on African culture; this means not that the diseases, or rather their symptoms, are seen as associated with African peoples only, but that their interpretation is bound up with African ways of viewing health and disease. What I find illuminating here is that a distinction is made between peoples native to Africa and those from countries overseas. Although Zulu are aware of the difference in culture and language between the different societies of African indigenous peoples, they nevertheless accept that there is an affinity between the different cultures regarding the world view which makes it possible for a Zulu medical practitioner to operate in a Sotho, or Pedi, or Shona or Thonga society, and vice versa.

Ecology and health

The ideas about the ecological influence on health are one instance of the causality of illness as interpreted within the scope of Zulu cosmology, which constitutes a second level of the operation of natural forces in the sphere of health and disease.

Zulu believe that there is a special relationship between a person and his environment, and that plant and animal life somehow affect the environment. As different countries or regions have different types of plants and animals, they therefore have different environmental and atmospheric conditions. The people in any particular region are adjusted to their surroundings; but should they go to a completely different region they would become ill, not being adapted to the new atmospheric and environmental conditions.

Zulu also believe that, when moving, both men and animals leave behind something of themselves, and absorb something of the atmosphere through which they move. It is this "something" left behind that is tracked down by dogs when hunting or when tracking a criminal. What is left behind in motion is known as *umkhondo* (track). Because neither men nor animals are restricted to a particular region, when they return from distant parts markedly different from Natal and Zululand, they bring back foreign elements that they have absorbed in their travels. Some wild animals and birds are reputed to travel long distances and on their return may introduce something foreign. In addition, poisonous snakes also leave dangerous tracks behind, and places where lightning has struck are also dangerous.

The word *umkhondo* is used mostly to describe a visible track on the ground. But it also describes the invisible track "picked up by dogs". If that is floating in the air, the correct term of reference is *imimoya*, not *imikhondo*. A person is said to "inhale *imimoya*" (*uhabula imimoya*) but "to step over *imikhondo*" (*weqa imikhondo*). Usually an adjective *emibi* (bad) is added to differentiate between harmless and harmful tracks, as such tracks are harmful only under special conditions. Since I use *imikhondo* in its harmful sense only, I think the adjective unnecessary in the present context. Furthermore, because the word *imimoya* can also mean spirits, air, wind, soul, as well as an amicable disposition of people, it is more convenient to use *imikhondo* for all tracks, whether in the air or on the ground. The implication here is that the undesirable elements in the atmosphere are picked up through inhalation or through contact either by touching or "stepping over" (*ukweqa*). In "stepping over" or contact by touching, the joints of the bone structure are said to be the most vulnerable points through which evil elements enter the body. Hence in prophylactic treatments incisions are made on the joints in order to introduce medicine directly into points where the body is most at risk.

Certain wild animal tracks (*imikhondo yezinyamazane*) are believed to affect infants, who, because they cannot walk, inhale them. However, owing to regular medication against *imikhondo* of wild animal track type, a baby gradually develops immunity and by the time it reaches childhood it is usually immune. But an adult can be a carrier of this type of *umkhondo*. A nursing or a pregnant mother can pick up such *imikhondo* and her baby becomes sick as a result. The figures given in Chapter 7 suggest that one factor often believed to be responsible for infantile mortality is the type of environmental disease contracted by pregnant or lactating mothers and passed on to their babies.

I have already mentioned that *umkhondo* specifically means "a track", but the action of contracting a disease by stepping over dangerous tracks is known as *umeqo* (n.) (*-eqa*, vb., to step over). All diseases contracted by stepping over something dangerous to health are known as *umeqo*, regardless of their symptoms. Whereas in the first level of natural causality (*imkhuhlane*) mentioned above the disease is identified by its symptoms, diseases associated with ecological dangers are identified primarily by the nature of causation rather than by the symptoms. The reasons for this logic will be clearer when I deal in more detail with treatment of disease. We shall then see the importance of identifying the cause of illness and correcting it. Treating the symptoms only would be ineffective if not done simultaneously with removing or correcting the source of illness; it would be like treating bilharzia symptoms while the patient continues to swim in an infested pool.

Ironically, the dangerous environmental situation can be aggravated by some of the methods used in the treatment of disease. It is believed that certain types of disease can be taken out of a patient and be discarded as a definite material substance; having been discarded it may hover around in the atmosphere or remain localized until it attaches itself to someone else. In this way what is removed when curing certain forms of disease renders the environment dangerous. It is said that, to keep the immediate environment clear, cross-roads (*enhlanganweni yezindlela*) and highways (*endleleni yomendo*) are popular places for the discarding of dangerous substances. Since these places are frequented by travellers, the undesirable substances would be attached to the latter and so be carried way from the territory.

The environment is not only polluted by undesirable tracks or by what is discarded in healing. It is also made dangerous by sorcerers, who place noxious substances on a particular person's pathway or scatter them along pathways to harm any passers-by, with a condition of *umeqo*.

In this way, the environment progressively becomes riddled with dangers. In order to survive despite these dangers, everyone must be frequently strengthened to develop and maintain resistance. In other words everyone must establish and maintain a form of balance with his surroundings. The balance is established not only between a man and his impersonal surroundings but also between man and man. If a person uses very strong medicines to establish this balance, when he meets someone who is not properly strengthened, the latter is overpowered by his presence and may become ill. This is known as *ukweleka ngesithunzi*, "to feel or suffer the weight of someone's overpowering influence". For this reason, people who live together are strengthened at the same time to keep up the balance between them.

There is no word in Zulu which means "balance". The notion is, however, implied in the word *lungisa* (vb. *lunga*) which Doke and Vilakazi translate as "to put in order, arrange, adjust, set as it should be, tidy" or *hlela*, vb., to put in order; *uhlelo*, n., the order, procedure, programme, state of being in order.

The word commonly used in this context is *ukuzilungisa*. It means to restore order where there has been disorder. In other words, I am using the English word "balance" to mean "moral order" in the symmetrical sense in relation to the position of people vis-à-vis other people, the environment, the ancestors and other mystical forces that produce pollution. "Balance" in this sense should be understood to mean "symmetry" or "order" rather than, as usual, the central pivot in a counterpoise situation.

The idea of order and disorder involving medicines is very well demonstrated by Callaway:

> There are medicines which give chiefs strength and presence; a common man, who is neither a chief nor a doctor, cannot touch this kind of medicine; if anyone among the chief's men were seen with it, he used to be killed; it was said, "What are you intending to do with that?" For a chief feels with his body a man who has great medicines; and when such a man stands in his presence he is oppressive; it is as though the chief was bearing him, and he feels a perspiration breaking out and he starts up and goes away to strengthen himself with medicines (*imuke iye kuzilungisa*). If that man does not leave these medicines he will die. The chief will say to him, "Son of so-and-so, if you do not leave off this conduct of yours, you are already dead. Give me all your medicines that I may see those which you have about you." And indeed the man does not conceal them, because he has been discovered by being felt by the chief's body. And if the chief finds a great medicine on him he asks what he does with it and from whom he got it. He says he purchased it from so-and-so. The chief asks what he was about to do with it, and he explains what he was going to do when he bought it; perhaps he says to make damsels love him. The chief takes the medicine and places it among his own.
>
> 1885, p. 417

The idea that a chief has a right to use stronger medicines to develop the "weight of his personality" persists. The medical practitioners know what "medicines" to use to strengthen the chief and what "medicines" are reserved for the people in general.

I have laboured this point of "balance" because it is the pivotal ideology around which revolve practically all the notions that constitute what is known as "African disease" (*Ukufa kwabantu*).

It will become clearer later on how crucial the idea of "balance" is in health matters. For a Zulu conceives good health not only as consisting of a healthy body, but as a healthy situation of everything that concerns him. Good health means the harmonious working and co-ordination of his universe.

Some people are considered much more vulnerable than others to environmental dangers. These are: infants, strangers in the territory, people who have allowed a long stretch of time to elapse between treatments, and finally persons who are considered polluted.

An infant is not only a stranger to the environment. It also has a fragile bone structure, with wide joints, such as the fontanelle (*ukhakhayi*), which is considered a weak point against the hazards of the environment. In order to survive, the baby must be protected even before it is born. Its mother must observe a pattern of behaviour that will minimize contacts with *imikhondo*.

The second category of people who are vulnerable to environmental or ecological dangers are strangers or "newcomers" in the area. The significance of this is well expressed by Van Gennep:

> The strangers must stop, wait, go through a transitional period, enter and be incorporated. . . . This isolation has two aspects which may be found separately or in combination: such a person is weak because he is outside a given group or society but he is also strong since he is in the sacred realm with respect to the group members for whom their society constitutes the secular world. . . .
>
> 1960, p. 26

Such a notion is true for the Zulu. The stranger is "strong and weak" in the sense that although he is regarded as having in himself strong dangerous foreign influences, he too is nevertheless in danger of the influences of a strange region. For this reason all newcomers in the Nyuswa reserve stay with a friend who is sponsoring them for about a period of three months. During this period the local people have an opportunity of observing them and deciding whether they are "dangerous" or not, and also whether they can be assimilated into their social life. Only after the period of probation, and when the people in the immediate neighbourhood have indicated their acceptance of the strangers, can they build their own homes. Once this is done they get a local practitioner to strengthen them and their homestead with local medicines in order to make them fit into the new environmental situation.

The local people can also endanger themselves if they allow long periods to elapse between strengthening treatments. Ideally the homestead and the inmates are strengthened once a year in spring. This is done to precede summer with its lightning thunderstorms, as the strengthening treatment also includes protection against lightning.

Some people put off the treatment until an incident suggests that there is need to strengthen themselves. This may be the destruction of property by lightning or sickness in the family.

People in a state of pollution include, for instance, the bereaved, the newly-delivered mother, the homicide, and menstruating women. All these are considered vulnerable to environmental disease.

Ecological factors are supposed to be the primary cause of a wide variety of illnesses, some minor, others fatal. A few examples, with the causes to which they are attributed, are given below.

When a baby cries continuously, or when it is fretful or shows general debility, it is said to suffer from *inyamazane*, i.e. the effects of a certain wild animal track. Green diarrhoea and white-coated tongue are said to be symptoms of contaminating lightning fumes arising from an area recently struck by lightning. The condition is known as *inyoni* (bird), as it is believed that lightning strikes in the form of a bird. Nettle rash is said to be due to contact with fresh dangerous snake tracks. It will be shown later that many miscarriages, still-births and infantile mortality are associated with the undesirable elements in the environment usually contacted by a pregnant or nursing mother and affecting the baby. In the case of adults, symptoms ranging from general debility of the body to possession by evil spirits, are associated with the lurking dangers in the environment.

3 | Sorcery *(Ubuthakathi)*

The principles operating in the relationship between people and their surroundings as discussed in the last chapter have far-reaching implications for social relations. For instance, the notion that human beings when in motion absorb certain elements of their immediate surroundings makes an opening for sorcery whereby a sorcerer is able deliberately to place harmful substances in situations which can harm particular people. This is the most common sorcery technique, said to be used mainly because it is the easiest. Since whatever is discarded from the system by the use of certain types of medicines must be deposited where it is not likely to harm members of the community, a sorcerer can plant it at a point where a particular person is likely to pass by, and if that person is not sufficiently immunized or strengthened he may fall sick.

The intention is the crucial point that labels an act as one of sorcery. It may well be that someone comes into contact with dangerous substances that have not been planted deliberately to harm anyone. In that case the person who placed these substances is not regarded as a sorcerer. To pursue this point further, let us take the case of nursing mothers. If they live in the same house, they must give strengthening medicines to their babies jointly; the first woman must invite the second's baby to participate, or else that baby on inhaling the medicinal fumes not intended for it will become ill. The woman would thus be considered to have practiced sorcery. But if she treats her baby without being aware that the second one is present in the house, this would not be considered as sorcery, even if the second baby falls ill as a result of the

uncontrolled fumes. It would be considered as an *umkhondo* or environ-
mentally dangerous influence picked up by accident.

Intention, however, operates within a framework of certain norms.
For instance, there are medicines believed to create or to maintain
love (*intando*). While men are regarded as having a right to use love
charms (*iziphonso*) to win the hearts of girls they court, women are
not expected to use such charms to win the hearts of men they fancy.
This extends to a marriage situation. In a polygynous society a man
should be free to pay his attentions to not only one but any of his wives
or prospective wives. But a wife who uses love charms is regarded as
selfish and possessive. It is further maintained that since she prepares
the husband's food she has ample opportunity of adding love medicines
to the food. This endangers his life, as his enemies are likely to sell
poisonous substances to his wives under the guise of love charms. If a
woman is found adding such substances to her husband's food, she is
considered as a sorcerer even though she may protest that her intention was not to kill him but to make him love her.

Closely associated with this notion is the right reserved for a husband
to use medicines to harm his wife's lover, who after having intercourse
with her develops a condition known as *iqondo*.[1]

Finally, self-protection is considered the right of everyone. Some
practitioners are believed to protect a homestead and its inmates with
measures calculated to make sorcery rebound on the sorcer. This is
considered morally acceptable.

A sorcerer is known as *umthakathi* (*abathakathi*, pl., *thakatha*, vb.). Three
types of sorcerers may be distinguished.

1. Night sorcery[2]

The first type is a "night sorcerer", who in many respects approximates
to the conventional concept of a "witch" as described for many African
societies, and especially by Evans-Pritchard for the Azande. Zulu
believe that such a sorcerer was "created or moulded with an evil
heart" (*Wabunjwa ngenhliziyo embi*). The stereotype is as follows. He

---

[1] Dr W. Z. Chonco, a Zulu Western-trained doctor, has written in an unpublished manuscript his clinical experience of this condition. He writes: "The most dreaded of men's diseases.
Localized—lower abdomen and genitals. Blanket name for: Prostatitis, prostatic enlargement with retention of urine, bilharzia, dysentery, epididymo-orchitis, and even intestinal
obstruction."

[2] All forms of sorcery are known as *ukuthakatha* and the sorcerer as *umthakathi*. A murderer is
known as *isigebengu*; so are the people who assault others in cold blood. They are not *abathakathi*.

harms people for no apparent reason. He keeps baboons as familiars. When he visits homesteads at night to perform his evil acts, he rides naked on these baboons, facing backwards. He digs up corpses, resurrects them, and out of them makes dwarfs (*imikhovu*) who are under his control. He uses them to till his fields at night, while most people are asleep, in order to be more successful and gain advantage over others. He is mean and jealous and tends to keep to himself. His chief technique is to scatter or bury noxious medicines in the homes of his victims. Because he is so thoroughly evil-hearted, on such nocturnal visits he also scatters medicines along the pathways to harm anyone who may pass by. He is a danger to the community at large and is feared. He may also, but not necessarily, observe the techniques of the two other types of sorcery mentioned below.

The "night sorcerer" is always a man. Although said to have been "moulded with an evil heart", he is aware of what he is doing and has conscious control over his actions. He always uses medicines, and even though he has some superhuman powers, such as his ability to resurrect corpses, he cannot fly, change shape, vanish, or perform similar feats usually associated with the powers of wizards. For these reasons he is better described as a sorcerer than as a witch. His aim, as his technique suggests, is to render the environment dangerous for his victim, or to put people out of balance with their environment. He may influence his son to become a sorcerer by incising the boy's rectum and rubbing medicines into the incision. This will give the boy an urge to practise sorcery.

The technique of placing harmful medicines is known as *umbhulelo*. This includes the medicines over which people "step", therefore contracting a condition known as *umeqo* (see above, p. 26). It also includes smearing harmful substances on to objects which the victim is likely to touch, such as a handle of a hoe or a plough or a stool. The harmful substances are believed to single out the victim if they have been mixed with his "body dirt" (i.e. his sweat, nails, or hair), or if his name is mentioned when they are placed. In such cases they harm the intended victim only. If there is no specific victim, anyone who is not properly strengthened can be harmed.

It is usually this type of sorcery which is given as a reason for the segmentation of extended homesteads (*inxuluma*). When a homestead has been on the same site for too long, the charms placed by "night sorcerers" are believed to accumulate and "charge" the site with sorcery. It may be of interest to observe that people usually become particularly sensitive to this after the death of a homestead head who within the homestead had either several wives or married sons and their families. It is customary to move to a new site after the mourning period is over and the sacrifice to integrate the dead man with the body of ancestors has been performed. Invariably when a change of site takes place, the sons of the deceased do not erect another extended homestead; instead, each son builds his own home independently, usually on the lineage land set aside for his wife's cultivation. The use of the notion of sorcery to bring about segmentation of a homestead has been analysed by Marwick (1952) in his material on the Cewa of Malawi. The difference is that among the Zulu it is not alleged sorcery within the homestead, but sorcery that comes from without, which is usually thought to lead to segmentation.

In the Nyuswa Reserve I knew five men who were said to be night sorcerers. Significantly they were all successful men according to Nyuswa standards. They were all self-employed; four were doctors (*izinyanga*), and the fifth had a successful diviner wife who usually had divination novices who helped in tilling the fields. All five men had cattle, and together they owned 74 of the 352 cattle (i.e. 21 per cent) in our sample of 100 homesteads (see above, pp. 20–21). This ownership of cattle not only demonstrated but also promoted their success. They had spans of oxen readily available to till their land and take advantage of the rainy season, while most people without cattle had to depend on them for assistance. They could be assured of a good crop as they had plenty of cattle manure; in addition, they had more time to develop their land, since they were not away on migrant labour. Their success was measured by the fact that their families did not starve, as they had access to *amasi* (curdled milk), a highly prized Zulu dish.

My impression was that these five men shared certain personality traits. They tended to be arrogant and generally treated other people with contempt.

In a society where a premium is placed on mutual assistance, sharing the good and bad things of life, it becomes understandable when people label as sorcers those who appear to be selfish and malicious. It is significant that several men as well off as the five cited here, were not necessarily so labelled—because they were not considered to be antisocial. Another point worth considering is the ambiguity of the term *umthakathi* (sorcery). It is sometimes used idiomatically to mean power. For instance a car that has a powerful engine is referred to as *umthakathi*, here understood to mean its power. In other words, although the five men were disliked, they were also feared for their power. I know of no nonentity who was regarded as *umthakathi* of this type.

The common factors shared by people believed to be night sorcerers are their personality qualities and their success. An additional factor was that the five men had access to medicine, which in the hands of an evil man could be used to do harm. There were, however, a number of other doctors who were not regarded as sorcerers.

It is significant, however, that, although diviners also have access to medicine, none of those in the Nyuswa reserve were suspected of sorcery. When inquiring about this, I was often told that the spirits which possess the diviners expect of them a high moral code. They would lose their clairvoyant powers if they used the medicines revealed to them to harm other people instead of helping them.

Writing of the Mpondo, Hunter (1961) sees the "night sorcerer" as a witch rather than a sorcerer. She points out that men and women are thought to have "familiars" with which they have sexual intercourse, and by means of which they legally destroy life and property. She calls such people "witches", in contrast with "sorcerers", who do not have familiars but only use harmful substances to destroy life. The most commonly used familiar among the Mpondo is *Thikoloshe*, "a small hairy being with prominent sex organs, which has attributes of making itself invisible". Another familiar commonly said to be possessed by women is *izulu* or *impundulu*. It is conceptualized as a mysterious bird which comes with lightning. It also has powers of becoming invisible and of changing into any form, usually that of a beautiful young man who becomes the lover of its possessor.

The Zulu know of these familiars, but regard them as Xhosa familiars which have been brought to Natal and Zululand either by Xhosa themselves or by Zulu migrant labourers who learn about them from Xhosa people in the town centres. I did not hear of anyone who was said to possess these familiars among the Nyuswa. The people who were regarded as night sorcerers were said to use the Zulu traditional familiars, i.e. the baboon (*imfene*) and the zombies (*imikhovu*).[1] These

---

[1] Another Zulu familiar which was said to be occasionally used by women is a cat (*impaka*). The notion of this familiar seems to be disappearing as I never heard it mentioned among the Nyuswa. When I mentioned it I was told that such an *impaka* is said to have been trained by women to steal certain articles from the co-wives in order to get hold of their body-dirt which was used to make the husband dislike them. However, no one was said to possess such an *impaka* among the Nyuswa.

have no power of making themselves insivible or of changing form. They operate usually in the company of their master at night to harm people. By day they are hidden and fed, because they are treated as physical beings. These differences between the Mpondo and Zulu concepts of familiars makes me hesitate to regard the Zulu night sorcerer as a witch. The Zulu word for such people is *abathakathi*, which I have translated as sorcerers. (Those who use potions to harm others do so deliberately.)

2. *Day sorcery*

The second type of sorcerer acts, not as a matter of habit, but only in cases of personal animosity. He may be regarded as a sorcerer not by the community at large, but only by those with whom he is in conflict. The main method he is said to use is *ukudlisa*, adding noxious medicines, including Western poison, to the victim's food. This may be supplemented by other techniques, such as placing harmful substances along the victim's path, or stealing important portions of a sacrificial beast with the object of not only nullifying the victim's sacrifice but also reversing its purpose. (The significance of these important portions will be shown later, when I discuss the treatment of disease.)

This class of sorcerers includes both men and women. But women are believed to be in the majority and understandably so, because (unlike men) they cannot be either "night sorcerers" or "lineage sorcerers" (see below).

"Day sorcery" occurs in situations rife with competition, jealousy and rivalry, such as may be found in a polygamous or extended family situation among wives or fellow-workers.

There is a well-known case in the Nyuswa area of suffering believed to have been brought about by a woman sorcerer who stole the chyme of the important marriage beast (*eyesikhumba*). This beast is calculated to establish the marriage and also make the wife fertile. The couple had nine children, but four died of what the Western doctors diagnosed as Hirchsprung's disease. Most of them died in spite of the operation. Many people believed that the hospital could not cope with the disease because it is an African disease (*ukufa kwabantu*), a result of sorcery which Western doctors could not possibly understand.

I have cited this case because it illustrates the belief that there are certain types of diseases that baffle the scientists. In other words the

Western type of treatment is put to a test and sometimes found in-
adequate. Therefore it does not differ very much from the traditional
treatment, which sometimes succeeds and at other times fails.

3. *Lineage sorcery*

Thirdly, there is the lineage sorcerer (*uzalo*). Members of a lineage
segment are descendents of a common grandfather. They share sacrifices
and have certain ritual and social obligations towards one another.
They are not supposed to practise either of the types of sorcery discussed
above against each other, because this would meet with the disapproval
of the ancestors. If, for instance, members of a lineage segment quarrel,
they must rectify it by performing the ritual of *ukuthelelana amanzi*,
"washing each other's hands," thereby washing away anger. This is
accompanied by a slaughter of a goat and sharing in a sacrificial
meal.

However, a man can persuade the ancestors to favour him and
abandon one or more other members of the lineage. This is sorcery of a
special kind which can only be practised by one homestead head
(*umnumzane*) against another of the same segment. The ritual involves
"the churning of black medicines" (*ukuphehla amanz'amnyama*) in
connection with the treatment of disease. This type of sorcery can be
practised only by people able to sacrifice in their own right. It can
therefore be practised by men only. Its effects are to deprive the victim
and his dependants of the protection of the ancestors and therefore
expose them to all kinds of misfortunes. The condition can be partially
inherited, in that the succeeding patrilineal generation would also be
without the protection of the ancestors of the grandfather generation.

Figure 3 is a diagram of a lineage segment within which lineage
sorcery was believed to operate. Number 23 in the diagram was
accused indirectly by No. 33, who had lost his father (No. 13) in 1969
and his 12-year-old daughter in 1970. Number 13 had been old and an
invalid. His state of ill-health was aggravated by drinking "gavine", a
locally distilled concoction. The lineage members agreed among themselves never to give him "gavine". Number 23 had a beer party at his
home; No. 13 came to it, and was served with "gavine". He left that
evening in a drunken state but never reached home. A search party was
organized by No. 23 who, being an *inyanga* (doctor), was the only able-
bodied man of his lineage at home. (The others were all migrant labourers.)

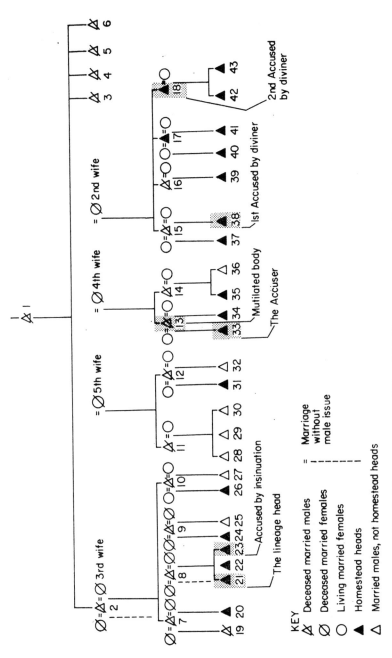

Fig. 3. Lineage segment within which lineage sorcery was believed to operate.

The missing man was found dead on the third day, a few hundred yards from No. 23's home. Across his chest lay a cord, which suggested strangulation. In addition, the body had been mutilated: the left leg had been amputated at the knee, the left eye and left testicle had been removed. Number 23 went to report the matter to the police and also to break the sad news to his agnates in town. The police, when they arrived at the scene of the tragedy, said No. 23 had reported that the body had been mauled by dogs.

In 1970, No. 33's 12-year-old daughter died. During her short illness (possibly while delirious) she called out No. 23's name and begged him not to kill her. She said she saw him coming towards her, holding a spear as if he was going to stab her. She was taken to the hospital. While on the way there by bus, she repeated her accusations, in the hearing of the Nyuswa passengers. She never reached hospital but died in transit.

Her father began to ask himself why No. 23 always seemed to be connected with his misfortunes. Number 23 had given "gavine" to No. 13 and had not bothered to see him safely home. He chose to tell the police that dogs had mutilated the body. But the most damaging factor was the dramatic death of the girl.

In self-defence No. 23 pointed out that during the beer party on the night of No. 13's disappearance, he had been called out on business to attend to a patient and had left the party in progress. In his absence his wife served "gavine" to No. 13, who by the time of his return had left. He could not therefore have been aware of No. 13's state of drunkenness. He denied ever telling the police that dogs had mutilated the corpse.

Number 33 was not convinced by these explanations. He approached No. 21, head of the lineage segment and a full brother of No. 23, to arrange with the lineage for an *umhlahlo*. *Umhlahlo* is a consultation with a diviner in cases of open accusations. Both the accuser and the accused agree upon the particular diviner who is to be consulted. She must be one who lives a good distance away and is therefore not known to either. Her methods of divination must be such that the consultants give no clue; they sit silently throughout the process of divination. Besides the accuser and the accused there must be neutral observers who represent the chief. These are chosen by the chief himself, and their duty is to report back to him and also to ensure that the protagonists do not fight.

The accuser in this particular case had not made an open accusation, but had implied a lot. When approaching the lineage-head, he had merely mentioned that in view of the unusual circumstances he would like all the heads of *imizi* of his lineage to accompany him to an *umhlahlo*. Seventeen lineage segment members went and two neutral observers. The diviner chosen lived more than 100 miles away. Cars for transport were hired.

The diviner said the deceased man had died of exposure because in his drunken state he slept in the open and had little resistance as an invalid. Nobody had killed him. But two men (whom she named) from the neighbouring chiefdom came upon the corpse by chance and mutilated it for their own nefarious purposes. Number 33 had experienced a series of misfortunes because he was a victim of *uzalo* (lineage sorcery) directed against his father's house and now his own, not by the man he suspected, but by No. 38 and No. 18, a "brother" and a "father", the first being the primary mover and the second his aid. They had been cunning in their practice of sorcery in that they always used *izicuyo* or *insila*, i.e. body "dirt" such as sweat of the suspected man. This explains why the child kept "seeing No. 23 coming to kill her".

This was an unexpected turn of events. Usually any person convicted at *umhlahlo* sessions is exiled along with his family, and this is enforced ruthlessly by burning down his home, looting, and beating him up. Very often he barely escapes with his life. The *umhlahlo* decision in this case was so unexpected that the accuser, No. 33, refused to accept it. He maintained that No. 23 had used "medicines" to confuse the diviner. As a result nothing happened to the men who had been found guilty by the diviner. As soon as the party returned to Nyuswa, the man originally accused went to the headman to lay a charge of libel against the accuser. The headman refused to consider the matter and said it was a lineage matter to be settled at a lineage level. It had not yet been settled in August 1971.

I have given a detailed account of this case, partly because I wanted to bring out more forcefully the notion of lineage sorcery, which has not been mentioned previously in anthropological literature on the Zulu, and also because the case illustrates different facets of the notion of sorcery.

Let us look first at the significance of the grading of siblingship in the lineage segment. Figure 3 will serve for illustrative purposes.

The present generation (Nos 19–43) are grandchildren of No. 2. He had five wives. According to traditional usage, if there are many wives they are divided into right and left sections (*umdlunkulu nekhohlo*). The first married wife, who is the chief wife (*umdlunkulu*), is the senior wife in the right-hand section, and the second wife (*ikhohlo*) is the senior wife of the left-hand section. Subsequent wives are alternated between the two sections. In this case, for instance, the third and the fifth wives belong to the right-hand section, while the fourth wife is on the left-hand section. If (as happened here) the first wife has no issue, the third wife produces the heir. In the present generation the leader of the lineage segment is No. 21, grandson of the third wife by her second son and his second wife. (Number 20, her grandson by her first son, is in fact senior to No. 21, but is mentally unstable.)

If we reconstruct No. 2's homestead, there was once within it himself and his five wives, his twelve sons and their twenty wives, and probably his young grandchildren.

When the sons of the four wives who bore male children married, each wife allocated fields to her daughter-in-law, cutting out pieces from her own fields. As a result her daughters-in-law had adjacent fields. The relevance of this is that when segmentation took place each son built his home on the field of his chief wife. Consequently the sons of one woman all built in close proximity. Figure 3 not only shows the siblings, but also reflects their geographical positioning. The homesteads stretch along the lineage plain in the chronological order beginning at one end with No. 20 and ending at the other extreme with No. 43. As the chart indicates the first and second wives occupy the right- and left-hand sides respectively of the lineage land, thereby establishing boundaries.

This grading of the siblings is not only demonstrated geographically, but is put into effect in social relations. For instance, assistance is expected first from uterine siblings, then from siblings of the side in which one belongs, and finally from those of the other side. The range of sibling nearness is manifested during funerary rites, weddings, and confinements.

What I want to bring out is that this arrangement indicates lines of conflict between the members of a sibling group. For instance, in the sorcery case the conflict expressed by the implied accusation is one of long-standing duration between the right-hand and left-hand side groups. It goes back to conflicts between No. 2's second and third wives. Quarrels have erupted and subsided over a long period between the two sides. The present quarrel was recognized by non-lineage members as a symptom of an old division. As lineage members the two sides socialized, drank together, and united against any outsider, but their reciprocal relationship was nevertheless not an easy one. However, they had never reached a stage in the past when they had to undertake a legal divination (*umhlahlo*). The instance of *umhlahlo* described above suggests a growing deterioration of relations.

The importance of this account is that it illustrates how conflicts that may exist between a man's wives may be passed on to the sons. After all, the sons of a woman grow up knowing, through their mothers, who their enemy is and what that enemy does. Serious differences between co-wives or wives of brothers may form the foundation of conflicts between the sons of those wives. While within the homestead sorcery accusation may be between women, when the homestead has segmented the conflicts may continue to smoulder, and if fanned by any clash between the sons of antagonistic women they may be translated into lineage sorcery.

Peters makes a very important point when he writes:

> When, therefore, a person is successfully accused of witchcraft the condemnation is of an act or acts lying in the general field of morality. Before making an accusation a man first considers who among his neighbours bears him ill-will, so that when an accusation is made it is tantamount to saying that this man's envy, malice, greed, and so on, is adversely affecting the social well-being of his fellow man.
>
> 1972, p. 142

Among the Zulu, before an open accusation is made, the truth of which can only be decided by a legal divination (*umhlahlo*), the accuser will have good reason to make the accusation. He will have privately consulted several diviners to confirm his suspicions. In addition he would be almost sure that general public sympathy was on his side.

In the case cited above, although there were incidents involving the accused which strengthened the accuser's suspicions, the latter was not quite confident of support from public sympathy. For this reason he was cautious. He made insinuations, but never a straightforward accusation. He must have realized that the man he suspected was popular, and did not conform to the stereotype notions of a sorcerer; although brilliant and perhaps cynical (which came out particularly during the tribal court sessions), he was not considered malicious. That he was not the type that could easily be associated with sorcery was superbly demonstrated in 1968. As a doctor he had given a purgative to one of the local young men. The latter did not follow his instructions, but took an overdose and died. People did not think he had killed the young man; even the bereaved family accepted that the death was accidental.

The diviner's verdict accused people who would not be affected by the accusation, in that they were the type of people "who could not harm a fly". The importance of the verdict in this case was that it exonerated the accused, and its accusation of the other people was ignored by the injured party as well as by the public In this sense this case supports Peters's observation.

The same observation, with a different slant, is made by Park (1967). He points out that divination has the function of eliminating the important source of disorder in social relations. It has the effect of stamping with a mark of special legitimacy a particular decision or a particular kind of response to crisis. The diviner is able in the public conscience to remove the agency and the responsibility for a decision from the actors themselves and to cast it upon the heavens—which in the case of the Zulu is the ancestral spirits.

In this way the Zulu lineage court or chiefly court is saved from passing judgement on sorcery issues, and responsibility is transferred to the diviner, whose decision is final. The person who is not favoured by the decision has no reason to complain, because he participates willingly and is free to choose the diviner to be consulted. The accused, if found guilty, accepts the fact that he has to leave the community. If he is exonerated, the accuser must compensate him. The nature of compensation is decided either by the lineage court if the accusation is within the lineage segment, or by the chiefly court if the protagonists do not belong to the same segment.

I must, however, emphasize here that open accusations are not lightly made. They are made only in situations where the relationship has deteriorated to an unbearable point. In most cases one of the parties decides to leave the area or move away from the neighbourhood. An accusation leading to a legal divination is thus avoided.

I shall now consider the sociological meaning of the three types of sorcery as seen by the people themselves.

A married woman's awareness of her position within the homestead of her affines is well dramatized by the *ukuyala*[1] custom. Just before leaving her home for that of her affines, the bride sits in a hut into which

---

[1] *Yala*, vb,. to warn, to put on one's guard. See also Krige on this (1930, p. 136).

her "mothers" come to give her their final instructions. She is told that in her new home she will be called by all sorts of names—she will be said, for instance, to be a thief, mean, lazy, and selfish. But above all she will be called a sorcerer. This should not worry her—she should endeavour to behave as well as she can. She must remember that she has gone to represent her lineage. She must never let whatever they call her come true. She must also remember that she is married not only to her husband but to his family. She must feed them, take an interest in what they are interested in, and respect them all. She must watch her tongue and never tell tales. She must be diligent and open handed, choose her friends with care, and make her mother-in-law her best friend. Usually the *ukuyala* ends with these words: *"Inkonzo enhle Nkosazana. Uze usikhonzele emzini:* Pay good homage our loving daughter. Pay respects to your new home on behalf of us all."

The point I am making here is that it is known and expected that a married woman, as an outsider, is usually regarded with suspicion by her affines and may even be thought of as a sorcerer. This is not only because she is a newcomer. It goes deeper than that, as the people themselves recognize.

I was told that in her affinal home (*emzini*) a married woman is only partially under the control of her husband's ancestral spirits, as his wife; as a daughter her own ancestors are still interested in her welfare. This is evidenced by the fact that if a married woman becomes a diviner she is possessed by the spirits of her own ancestors, not by those of her husband. While men of a lineage group are enjoined by religious sanctions not to practise sorcery on one another or on the women who bear the children for the lineage, wives are not controlled by these sanctions. It follows that the religious sanctions are believed to be much more effective than the secular sanctions, since the latter depend on proof and evidence while the former operate automatically. According to this ideology, it is only women married into the homestead who are potentially sorcerers, as they do not have to fear reprisals from its ancestors.

It was further pointed out that within a homestead the people who are likely to be rivals for a husband's recognition or a mother-in-law's friendship are a man's co-wives or the wives of brothers. Their rivalry and resentment provide areas of envy, jealousy, hatred and conflicts, all of which are believed to be the source of sorcery.

When I asked whether a man never resents his wife or quarrels with her, I was told that a man can always beat his wife if she errs or send her home to be further instructed, or marry another woman if he chooses to.

A woman sorcerer was said to use mainly a technique of adding harmful substances to the victim's food. This she can easily do because she handles food and she only intends to harm a particular person with whom she is in conflict.

Night sorcery, it was pointed out, is physically impossible for a woman because it entails training a baboon, digging up corpses to make zombies and visiting the homes of the victims at night. The only people who go about at night as they please are men. No man would tolerate a wife who disappeared at night. A man as head of the homestead, is free to keep baboons and zombies as he wishes, and order his wives to feed them.

Lineage sorcery, too, can only be practised by men, because they are the ones who invoke ancestors.

Two forms of sorcery are thus impossible for women, viz. lineage sorcery and night sorcery. Yet a man is able to practise all three forms, including the one particularly attributable to women. This is said to be especially the case in the work situations of the present day.

What this suggests is that men are generally expected to use sorcery techniques in their position as homestead heads to harm other homestead heads and their dependants, whereas women practise sorcery to harm the particular people they are in conflict with. In other words sorcery operates along structural lines.

This indigenous sociological interpretation indicates that Zulu are aware of a relationship between sorcery and the nature of the structure of the society, the roles that people play, and the religious beliefs which operate.

It also indicates the paradoxical situation created by the pattern of social structure, because it is the situations which generate competition, envy and jealousy that are associated with sorcery. Situations of this nature are found between co-wives; between brothers who are homestead heads with unequal fortunes; between homestead heads who are unrelated neighbours but whose fortunes are also not the same. Sorcery as a notion in this sense expresses the imbalance inherent in the social structure itself—the imbalance that carries within itself seeds of evil.

What has also emerged from this account is that sorcery as a concept paradoxically indicates the external corporateness of units and at the same time also points at the internal division.

That the lineage members within a homestead may not practise any form of sorcery indicates the unity of the homestead, but that wives are likely to practise sorcery within it is a pointer to its internal division.

That homestead heads who are descendants of the same grandfather, and who describe themselves as "eating together" (*sidla ndawonye*), may not practise the usual forms of sorcery against one another underlines their structure as a corporate group; but that they are likely to practise lineage sorcery against each other indicates internal division of the lineage segment.

That the descendants of a great-grandfather who regard themselves as lineage members that "no longer eat together" (*asidlindawonye*), but are nevertheless united by agnatic ties and support each other in faction fights against other lineages, may practise sorcery of the ordinary kind against each other indicates not only the internal segmentation within the lineage but also the distance between such segments.

Finally, that the members of a community are expected to keep the locality clear of "pollution" by discarding dangerous stuff on frequented pathways and crossroads, so that travellers and outsiders may carry it away elsewhere, underlines the corporateness of the community as a local unit (it also combines in faction fights against other communities); but that night sorcerers are a menace within a community indicates internal segmentation.

There is yet another paradox in the operation of sorcery. The ancestors who are considered custodians of one's destiny are sometimes persuaded by the very descendants they protect to abandon one of their number.

We have, however, a very suggestive biblical parallel in the story of Isaac, whose younger son, Jacob, used stealth to get the blessing that was reserved for the older son, Esau. When Esau arrived later for the blessing, he found that Isaac had already unwittingly given it to Jacob and could not retrieve it for him. This did not mean that Isaac did not love Esau, only that Esau had been outwitted by his brother Jacob.

Likewise, all things being equal the ancestors are believed to be good and loving towards all their descendants who, being equal, feel equally entitled to ancestral care and protection. But in reality they realize that their fortunes are not the same. In such cases they feel cheated, not by their ancestors, but by the wicked, envious, greedy and jealous brothers, who, like Jacob, get the ancestral blessing by stealth.

The important point here is that it becomes difficult for a dutiful man to explain why he suffers misfortunes when he is entitled to ancestral protection. But if the ancestors have been caused to abandon him by the wickedness of mankind, then they are absolved from blame.

The same may be said of sorcery practised by stealing vital sacrificial portions. That the purpose of the sacrifice is not realized is blamed on the sorcerer, not on the inability of the ancestors to respond favourably. The conclusion follows that the belief in sorcery, and the Zulu theory of its modes of operation, are necessary for the maintenance and internal consistency of the Zulu ancestral religion.

4 | The Ancestors and Illness

Before looking into the activities of the ancestors, I want to consider the other "Beings" in the "other world" and inquire to what extent they come into the picture of health and disease. Zulu say that in the beginning there was *uMvelinqangi* (the first Being).[1] At some point there was also *uNomkuhbulwane* or *Inkosazane* (the Princess).[2] At another, a reed growing on a river bank burgeoned and gave birth to a man. (No mention is made of a woman in relation to that man.) The people multiplied. *uMvelinqangi* sent a chameleon (*unwabu*) to tell them that "they will not die". After some time *uMvelinqangi* sent a lizard (*intulo*) to tell them that "they will die". The lizard overtook the chameleon, which had stopped on the way to feed on *ubukhwebezane*, wild mauve berries. When the chameleon at last arrived with the message that "people will not die", they refused to accept it, and decided to stick to the message already delivered by the lizard (*Sibambelentulo*). Meanwhile the *Inkosazane* promoted every fertility of the land, the people and the animals. Ideally every year in spring certain rites should be performed by married women and maidens to ensure good crops, more cattle and more healthy babies. These rites are directed to *Inkosazane*. *uMvelinqangi* is approached only in situations of catastrophe or impending disaster such as extreme drought, in which case both men and

---

[1] See also Callaway (1884, pp. 1–5) and Krige (1968, pp. 179–184).

[2] Rituals for *Inkosazane* are occasionally performed within the Valley of a Thousand Hills in Natal. Although people know of a ritual for *uMvelinqangi*, I have never met anyone who has participated in it.

women participate. Although *uMvelinqangi* is thought of as living "above" and does not normally affect the health or the life of an individual in day-to-day situations, there is nevertheless a "mystical force" which is closely associated with him, as we shall see in the next chapter.

In considering the relationship between people and their ancestral spirits, I shall begin by relating briefly four cases of illness associated with the ancestors.

CASE 1 Thuli, who belonged to the Phewa lineage, was made pregnant by a man who was not prepared to marry her, but only paid damages (i.e. an ox for Thuli's father, a cow for her mother, a goat for girls of her age group, another goat to cleanse them of defilement, and £5 as a fine to the chief for committing a wrong in the community). After the baby's birth, Thuli's father slaughtered a goat (*imbeleko*) to thank the ancestors for the safe delivery, and also to ask them to protect the baby (a boy named Mandla). The baby was in this way adopted by Thuli's parents. He grew up calling them "father" and "mother" and regarding Thuli as a sister. Thuli later got married to someone else. Mandla grew up and in due course also married. Soon afterwards he established his own home and took his genitor's name, Mvubu. This he did against the advice of all his relatives, who pointed out that one does not simply change a name without implicating the ancestors in the process. He soon experienced misfortunes. His first child died. His second child, a boy of 8 years, suffers from a disease that makes him unable to use his lower limbs; he is partially paralysed and spends most of the time as a patient in hospital. Mandla himself after 9 years of marriage became ill with swollen feet, and died early in 1970 at the age of 32. His illness was said to be a result of harmful substances smeared on the tools he used at work. Although he is believed to have died of sorcery, his death and his child's illness are associated with the lack of ancestral protection. His mother (his genitrix) concluding the account said: "Mandla was stubborn unto death. If he had heeded our advice he would still be alive."

CASE 2 MaDladla was married in May 1968. Her parents had performed the nubility rites (*ukwemula*) for her two elder sisters before they married. But in her case the rites were not performed, as her father had suffered a financial set back and his cattle had diminished in number. After two years of marriage she had not yet conceived. Her husband went to a diviner to ascertain the cause. He was told that MaDladla's ancestors were annoyed by the omission of the nubility rites, and when she got married, came along with her, and their presence around her created a "heaviness" (*bayesinda*) which stopped her from conceiving.

This was reported to MaDladla's father, who arranged to fetch the ancestors from his daughter's affinal home. He slaughtered a goat to propitiate the ancestors for the omission. He took the gall bladder of the goat and an old stick that had been used by his late father. He also provided himself with a green branch of *umlahlankosi* (a tree whose branches are used to place on a chief's grave). With these three objects he went to his daughter's affinal home, went to her own hut, told the ancestors that he had come to fetch them, and lightly struck the thatch with the stick. He sprinkled the gall on the *umlahlankosi* branch, all the time addressing his ancestors. He then pulled the branch behind him while returning home. On arriving, he entered the main hut and placed the branch, the stick and the gall bladder at the upper part of the hut (*umsamo*) where the sacrificial goat's meat was hanging.

Later MaDladla was invited by her parents to come home, and a goat known as *eyezinkobe*, which usually replaces the elaborate nubility rites, was sacrificed to enable her to conceive by fulfilling the fertility rites demanded by her ancestors.

CASE 3 Gwala, whose wife had given birth to twins, a boy and a girl, consulted a diviner because of the sudden illness of the baby boy. The diviner said that the baby was sick because Gwala's ancestors were angry and had withheld their protection of the baby. She emphasized that it was not the baby's maternal ancestors who were angry, as they were satisfied with the procedure that had been followed concerning them. Gwala, who had not sacrificed to his ancestors when his wife came to his family, had sacrificed only when the twins were born. The baby was ill because the ancestors were asking Gwala who the mother of the twins was. The diviner stressed that the medicines she was giving him to cure the illness would have no effect unless Gwala made peace with the ancestors by admitting guilt and promising to put matters right as soon as he possibly could.

The following is Gwala's background story. He was the eldest son and head of his family, as his father had died. His mother had a stroke and was paralysed. When this happened he was already half way with his marriage payments. Since there was no adult female in the house to nurse his mother, the girl's family was persuaded to allow her to live at his home while he collected enough money to cover the final wedding arrangements. The girl's father appreciated the difficult situation in which Gwala found himself and agreed. But before she left home, her father sacrificed and reported to the ancestors the circumstances surrounding her departure. This is what the diviner meant when she emphasized that the baby's maternal ancestors were satisfied because they had been given the respect which they considered their due. Gwala had missed out on this when he failed to report the circumstances surrounding the arrival of his future wife before the wedding ceremony.

CASE 4 This case is concerned with a difficult birth. The woman in labour had her own home, near that of her parents. Her mother-in-law, who lived a distance away, had come to be with her during her delivery. When she was in labour her chief midwives were her mother-in-law and her own mother. When the labour became protracted, there was concern for the lives of both mother and baby. At this point the two chief midwives armed themselves with sticks, went outside the hut, and beat the thatched roof with the sticks, calling upon the ancestral midwives to do their duty: "Do you want this baby to die? Why are you sitting there doing nothing?" The ancestral midwives so addressed were said to be the paternal grandmother of the confined woman and of her husband. After the baby had been born, two house lizards (*izibankwa*) showed their heads between the mud wall and the thatched roof. One of the midwives in the house said, "There they are, look at them, now they are rejoicing and are looking at the baby". The ancestral midwives were believed to have materialized as house lizards.

To understand the thought patterns behind these cases it is necessary to look into how the ancestral cult operates.

There are many words to denote the dead. *Amathongo* is a collective term for all the departed spirits. *Izithutha* means in particular spirits that have materialized as snakes or house lizards. (Usually male ancestors materialize as snakes, while female ancestors, particularly old women, materialize as house lizards.) *Izithunzi* (*isithunzi*, sing.) means "shadows". A shadow is believed to depart from the body when a person dies. A dead body is believed to cast no shadow. A shadow in this sense can be seen as synonymous with a soul, in that it is believed to depart from the body in the form of the body, although invisible. A dead person is initially an *isithunzi* until a sacrifice is performed after a period of mourning. The sacrifice integrates him with the body of the ancestors and also brings him back home as an *idlozi*. *Amadlozi* (*idlozi*, sing.) are the ancestral spirits responsible for protecting or disciplining the descendants. The term refers in particular to the spirits with jural powers over the descendants. *Abaphansi* means simply those who are down below, for the dead are believed to live "down below"—beneath the earth. It is synonymous with *amathongo*, as it refers to all the dead who belong to the family. The terms most commonly used by Nyuswa in everyday speech are *abaphansi* and *amadlozi*.

The ancestors are said to be primarily concerned with the welfare of their descendants. When good things of life are realized people say, "The ancestors are with us" (*Abaphansi banathi*). When misfortunes happen they say, "The ancestors are facing away from us" (*Abaphansi basifulathele*), for the ancestors are believed to withdraw their protection and gifts of good fortune from erring descendants. Without their protection the descendant's become vulnerable to all sorts of misfortune and disease.

People distinguish between ancestors that can punish or reward and ancestors that are powerless to do this. A man's mother, father, father's mother, and father's father are the most important ancestors. His father's brothers are next in importance, as they are believed to share in the sacrifice offered to parents and grandparents. But they do not act independently of the latter. These are patrilineal ancestors to whom a man sacrifices as a homestead head (*umnumzane*) (see p. 59).

The non-effective ancestors, who do not punish or reward as they have no jural powers over the living are those three generations or more removed from the homestead head. They nevertheless participate freely as guests of the effective ancestors. They are regarded as having a wide range of descendants, and they are free to be present at sacrifices by any one of them. Although they have no jural rights, such ancestors may possess a diviner, usually not as a leading spirit but as a supporting one. The spirits of people who die as minors, e.g. children and the unmarried, live with their elders in the spirit world and accompany them on sacrificial occasions.

Each child is placed under the protection of the ancestors by a sacrifice of a goat known as *imbeleko*[1] (*beleka*, vb., to carry on the back. The skin of the goat is usually prepared to be used to wrap the baby on its mother's back). Sometimes the goat is referred to as *eyeziphandla* (*isiphandla* is the wrist skin-band). This goat provides the first wrist skin-band for the baby. By this sacrifice the ancestors are thanked for, and also requested to protect the baby. It is a form of "baptism" which puts

[1] It is said that in former times, when there were wars, some children were abandoned. Such children were adopted through the sacrifice of *imbeleko*.

the baby under the protection of a definite range of ancestors. Ideally the *imbelekao* sacrifice is performed as soon as possible, within the first year of the baby's life. It is through an *imbeleko* sacrifice that social parenthood is established. Case 1 exemplifies this. Mandla was adopted by his mother's parents through an *imbeleko* sacrifice and was given the same range of ancestors as his mother, who then became his sibling. When he got married he decided to change his name and assume that of his genitor (Mvubu). In doing this he overlooked the importance of the *imbeleko* sacrifice. Mvubu's ancestors did not know him and therefore could not protect him, even if he called upon them when he sacrificed. This could have been rectified if Mvubu in addition to damages had paid an ox to get custody of the baby. He would then have put the baby under the protection of his ancestors even though not married to its mother. Mandla as an adult could still have rectified the situation by paying the extra ox to his mother's brother (or social brother), as his mother's father (or social father) was then dead. If his mother's brother accepted the ox, Mandla could then have asked Mvubu to introduce him to the ancestors by an *imbeleko* sacrifice.

Normally the children of a homestead head marry before he dies. When his son's baby has an *imbeleko* sacrifice performed, it is placed under the protection of its grandfather's ancestors, because the grandfather is the homestead head and performs the sacrifice. These ancestors protect the homestead head and all his dependants. When, however, the baby attains the status of sacrificing to the ancestors as a homestead head, he will be sacrificing to his own father and grandfather, his mother and father's mother, people who, under normal conditions, would all have been alive during his infancy and his youth.

A baby is protected in the patrilineal line by its paternal grandfather's ancestors. The protection it receives from the maternal ancestors is not identical in nature.

A girl's father is responsible for ensuring that her fertility rites are carried out. A married couple's first baby is given an *imbeleko* sacrifice (first sacrifice) by both groups: first by its father's group, and then by its mother's, when she takes it to her own parents, who sacrifice to thank the ancestors for having made their daughter fertile. Later babies are given an *imbeleko* sacrifice by their father's people only, and not also by their mother's. In other words the ancestor of the baby's mother are thanked at the first birth, and not again subsequently, for demonstrating that she is reproductive and had been worthy of marriage.

The baby's maternal ancestors are more interested in its mother, their daughter. But since the baby is the product of her fertility, for which they are responsible, they are also interested in the baby, and can cause harm to demonstrate that they control the mother's fertility. This explains case 2 where a woman whose nubility rites had not been performed could not conceive.

This case is of particular interest as demonstrating that the maternal ancestors do not only interfere with a woman's fertility in order to exert pressure on the affinal group and coerce them into fulfilling marriage-exchange obligations, but that they also exert such pressure to ensure fulfilment of what is due to them from their own descendants. For how could they be expected to make the woman fertile without having been requested to do so through a sacrifice?

The case also demonstrates that the place of a wife's ancestors is at her parental home, and not at her marital home. There can be no equal range of ancestors in one home (except in the case of diviners who achieve this by certain sacrifices.

Case 2 stands in contrast to case 3, where the paternal ancestors, angered by their descendants over marriage obligations, manifested their anger through the illness of the baby. The ancestors wanted to know who the mother of the twins was. I must mention here that sperm is likened to the seed sown in a woman's womb. The fruits of the seed belong to the sower. Hence, while a woman's ancestors are interested in her as a daughter and in her ability to reproduce, her husband's ancestors are interested in her as their wife and in what she reproduces as a mother. In this case Gwala had never introduced his wife to his ancestors, but had only presented them with the twins; accordingly they made one of the twins ill, to remind him to observe first things first. How could he expect them to protect the twins when he had failed to place under their protection the womb from which the children came?

Cases 3 and 4 highlight the position of a married woman in relation to the ancestors in her life. She stands astride—as a daughter to one group, and as a wife and mother to the other.

As a daughter she takes her first child to be given an *imbeleko* sacrifice by her parents. When she is bereaved by losing either a child or a husband, she is ceremoniously cleansed by her affines and then goes home to be cleansed by her own people. If she had contracted an illness before her marriage, she goes home to get it cured when it recurs. If she

misbehaves, say by committing adultery, she is sent home to her parents
to be taught once again how to behave, and she is expected to return
with a live goat from them which her affines sacrifice to appease their
ancestors. If her parents (or brothers) slaughter a beast that was given
for her *lobolo* (*amabheka*) she is entitled to a flank (*umhlubulo*) of the
meat, which she takes back to share with her affines. (Her son is entitled
to this portion if she is no longer alive.) When her daughter's nubility
rites are performed, her brother (or father, if still alive) contributes a
live goat. This is presented by her husband to his ancestors as a gift
from the celebrant's mother's people (*omalume*) to help to promote her
fertility. The gall is sprinkled on the girl, and she wears the inflated
gall bladder on her head as an indication of her maternal uncle's good
wishes. When a youth begins marriage negotiations the ideal negotiator
is his mother's brother, who also plays a leading role in the ritual on the
wedding day.

As a wife to her husband's people, a woman shares sacrifices with
them. She is equally affected by lineage sorcery directed against her
husband's group. If she falls ill as a married woman, it is the duty of her
affines to give her the necessary treatment; this may even mean a
sacrifice to the ancestors to procure her recovery. As she grows older,
she becomes progressively more identified with her affinal group and
less with her own people. After her menopause she is not expected to
observe the avoidance (*hlonipha*)[1] laws. She may, for instance, pro-
nounce words that are similar to the names of her senior male affines, or
even use the names themselves. But the most significant token of her
acceptance is that she may eat the special portion of meat (*inanzi*)—the
third stomach (caecum)—of the sacrificial animal set aside for the
ancestors. After her death she is brought back by a sacrifice as a mother,
never as a daughter to her own people. By this time the transfer from
her group of ancestors to that of her affines is complete.

This leads us to examine the degree of harshness shown by certain
ancestors towards their descendants.

---

[1] *Hlonipha* is an act of respect. In the above context it is used in relation to the behaviour
pattern of married women who, in conversation, avoid the use of words which contain the
radical of the name of certain persons, such as all those who are in the category of father-in-
law or grand-father-in-law. For example, if a woman's father-in-law is Thomas she will never
call anybody who is Thomas by name. In addition, she will avoid using words such as
atom, Tom, tomatoes, tomorrow, mass, massive, Mars, etc. She usually invents special names
for things and those who live with her gradually become able to understand her vocabulary.
In some instances there are certain *hlonipha* terms which are standardized, e.g. *Mpisholo* is a
hlonipha term for *mnyama* (darkness), *Mkhapheyana* for *umfana* (boy), etc.

Every person who dies has a sacrifice performed after the period of mourning, in order to integrate him with the rest of the ancestors. The deceased is believed to live alone away from the other dead spirits (*amathongo*) and away from home. A person who becomes an effective ancestor, i.e. who has jural rights to punish or reward, is the one who had such jural rights while alive. To such persons a sacrifice known as *ukubuyisa* is performed (*buya*, vb., come back; *buyisa*, bring back). If the deceased was a man a goat and an ox are sacrificed, if a woman a goat and a cow. If the deceased was unmarried and therefore a minor, a goat suffices, and the sacrifice is not referred to as *ukubuyisa*, calculated to bring the deceased home as such; it is calculated rather to integrate him with the body of the ancestors, in which case he comes home in their company. The ancestors concerned are particularly annoyed if the performance of this sacrifice is overdue. If a parent, he is said to come home in anger and bring chaos and a series of misfortunes. Such an ancestor is said to be the harshest. Harshness is not necessarily associated with the sex of the ancestor, but it is associated with the gravity of the wrong.[1]

I must point out here that the ancestors are thought of as withdrawing their protection if they are angered as a group. Without their protection a person is exposed to all dangers. In this sense they are not directly responsible for a death that may be brought about by other factors, because in the absence of their protection a person is vulnerable to sorcery and other environmental dangers as well as being prone to accidents.

Krige writes: "The spirits of old women and infants are often specially invited to come and eat a sacrificial meal, because the spirit of an old woman is supposed to be spiteful and malicious and capable of all sorts of harm, while that of an infant is pure and beneficent" (1950, p. 95). The Nyuswa in reply to this suggestion pointed out that the old woman is usually malicious in the context of an overdue *buyisa* ceremony. As a parent she can afford to be harsher to her children and even to her husband, but the children's spirits cannot do this outside the context of the ancestors who are their seniors.

The *buyisa* or integration ceremony is closely related to the first

---

[1] If the deceased was a parent the mourning period for the widow is usually one year. The *ukubuyisa* ceremony is supposed to be performed during the course of the year following the mourning year. Before *ukubuyisa* the deceased has no powers to bless the living, but may disturb them.

sacrifice, the *imbeleko*. The two are held for every person whether young or old, married or single. The *imbeleko* sacrifice identifies him as an individual, gives him a place as a member of a particular lineage, and also puts him under the protection of a definite range of ancestors. The *ukubuyisa* sacrifice integrates the spirit with its ancestors and other spirits of the lineage segment, and gives it a right to come home again as a spirit. The most significant point is that if a baby dies before the *imbeleko* sacrifice has been performed it cannot be integrated with the ancestral spirits through an *ukubuyisa* sacrifice. This was forcefully brought home to me by a woman who had lost her twins as infants. The first died soon after birth, and the second seven months later owing to burns. Explaining the cause of death she said of the first twin: "It travelled in a long journey back to where it came from". (In Zulu this is rendered in one word: *lenda*.) When twins die very young they are said to *enda* (travel); this term is reserved for twins only. Usually the death of a twin is not associated with any of the other causes. But when one twin has *enda*, or *endile*, the other is expected to live, particularly if it has out-grown the infancy stage. In this particular case the twin that lived had not yet been given the *imbeleko* sacrifice. To explain the cause of death (obviously due in fact to being burned by boiling water), his mother said: "He had not been given the *imbeleko* goat. His sister who *enda* was lonely and she fetched him so that she would have company. This happened easily because he was not a full person (*wengakabi umuntu*, not yet a person) as he had no *imbeleko*." There was no sacrifice to integrate both twins with their ancestors. I subsequently found that this was a widely held notion. It means that an infant is "made a person" by an *imbeleko* sacrifice, and being a person can then be integrated with the rest of the dead. No explanation is given regarding the whereabouts of those who die before *imbeleko*. It is usually said: "They return where they came from".

This leads to the question: Where are the ancestors supposed to be? I have already mentioned that, as a body of *amathongo*, they reside "down below", underneath the earth. This is their base, and from there they come to earth and live as an invisible section of the society.

During sacrifices the paternal ancestors, their guests (i.e. the spirits of the sacrificer's father's brothers and their wives), and the deceased minors of the family, congregate in the main hut. This hut belongs to the most senior woman of the group, who may be the widowed mother or the senior wife of the homestead head. It is the hut in which the belongings of the ancestors are kept, goats are sacrificed, and guests are received, and it is generally the centre of social life in the homestead. It is usually referred to as the "great hut" (*indlu enkulu*). The upper part of the floor is marked off by an inch-high ridge forming a semi-circle known as *umsamo*. No stranger may go beyond the ridge into the *umsamo* area, for it is here that the offering to the ancestors is made by burning incense; the beer set aside for ancestors is kept here and the sacrificial meat hangs here overnight—the beer is to be sipped and the meat licked or eaten by the ancestors.

The ancestors are also believed to rest on the rafters. This is well demonstrated by cases 2 and 4. It is further exemplified at divination sessions in cases of diviners possessed by the whistling ancestors (the great ancestors, *amakhosi amakhulu*). They whistle and converse directly with their clients from the rafters, particularly above the *umsamo* area.

The cattle byre is another place frequented by the ancestors, and sacrifices of oxen are always performed within it.

Besides these particular areas, the ancestors are believed to go about like all other people within the homestead. Outside the sacrifice situation, only the dead who particularly belong to the home are believed to be within. They are also believed to be simultaneously at different places. For instance, a deceased man with many married sons has a *buyisa* ceremony performed by all of them, and is expected to be at each home after each son has performed it. The same notion prevails with regard to possession. While a married diviner is possessed by her ancestors, they are at the same time believed to be at her parental home.

This leads us to examine the different modes of interaction between ancestors and their descendants. The ancestors that possess a diviner are essentially her own paternal ancestors. If her maternal ancestors, such as her mother's father or mother's mother, appear to her at all in dreams, they are usually on the fringe. The principal ones are always her paternal ancestors. These are not conceived of as taking possession of her and talking through her; they are thought of as sitting on her shoulders and whispering into her ears.

The problem arises when the possessed girl gets married or when she becomes possessed while she is married. There then arises a clash in the range of ancestors within the homestead. To resolve it the husband sacrifices a goat to his ancestors and requests them to allow the diviner's ancestors to operate within the homestead. If this is not done she never divines there.

If the husband wants to benefit from the proceeds of her divination, he shoulders the expense of her training as a diviner. (These are a series of goat sacrifices culminating with an ox sacrifice when her training is completed.) But if when she marries him she is already a diviner, and had had her expenses paid by her father, she gives her earnings to the latter. To redeem the situation the husband pays her father an ox. I know of one diviner whose husband refused to observe this procedure. She always went back to her home, which was close by, to meet her clients. She gave her earnings to her widowed mother, who was also a diviner. The mother reserved the right to dispose of the money as she wished; she occasionally gave it to her daughter as a present. She also provided her daughter with the goats necessary for the constant sacrifices made by diviners. Since sacrifice is a means of establishing closer contact with the ancestors, a diviner sacrifices much more often to promote and maintain her special contact with the ancestral spirits.

Incidentally, this notion also operates in the case of lineage sorcery. If a man destroys all or most of his agnates, the ancestors will focus on him, and their constant presence would put him in the same position as the diviner, in that he would have to sacrifice oftener to recognize their presence. For this reason, lineage sorcery if practised indiscriminately may boomerang, in that illness may result from the heaviness caused by the excessive spiritual contact. Such heaviness may only be allayed by constant sacrifice.

The question that arises is: Do the ancestors ever show their positive behaviour? To arrive at an answer it is important to look once more at the notion of "balanced" relationships. The world is thought of as basically good with the people and ecology blending together in harmony, and all things being equal the people get the necessary blessings from the ancestors to enable them to maintain the balance in their lives. As long as a man has a relatively successful life, i.e. has good relations within his family and with his fellow men, and a satisfactory economic situation, he considers himself as enjoying adequate protection and blessings from his ancestors. That is to say the ancestors normally bestow blessings, and withdraw them in exceptional instances only.

The ancestors are thanked from time to time by a sacrifice known as *ukubonga*, thanksgiving.

The following is a list of the different types of sacrifices, some of which have already been mentioned, that usually mark definite occasions.[1]

---

[1] Except for *imbeleko* for the first child only, which is offered by both groups to their respective ancestors, i.e. the infant's father's ancestors and the infant's mother's ancestors, whereby a

1. *Imbeleko* A goat, which is the first sacrifice offered for a baby and which places it under the protection of lineage ancestors.
2. *Ukubuyisa* A goat and an ox if the deceased was a married man, a goat and a cow if the decesaed was a married woman, a goat only if the deceased was a minor. The sacrifices integrate the deceased with the rest of the body of ancestral spirits.
3. *Ukubonga* A goat or an ox, to thank the ancestors for good things of life, e.g. a good win at the races, or a good job, or a generally satisfactory life.
4. *Ukucela izinhlanhla* A goat, to ask for the blessings of the ancestors before undertaking any major or risky task, e.g. before going out to major cities to seek employment.
5. *Ukushweleza* A goat, to appease the ancestors if there is evidence that they had been annoyed.
6. *Ukuthetha* A goat sacrificed to "scold" the ancestors if misfortunes continue to happen in spite of all efforts made to put things right.
7. *Ukukhomba inxiwa* A goat to show the ancestors "the new home" if the descendants move house.

These are the usual types of sacrifice which a homestead head (*umnumzane*) is likely to have performed during his lifetime.

There are, however, some occasions when a man slaughters a goat or an ox not for purposes of sacrifice but for general feasting.

The question that arises is how does an onlooker decide whether the killing is sacrificial or just for feasting? Since each sacrifice has particular rituals appropriate to its nature, it would not help to suggest that an onlooker should watch out for such rites, excepting one in particular that runs through all sacrifices. This is the use of the gall. The ancestral spirits are said to have a particular liking for the taste of gall. It is therefore always used specifically in order to achieve a special contact with them. It is always sprinkled on certain people to single them out for spiritual contact. I shall look more closely into the importance and significance of the bile later on.

Of those illnesses and deaths which are attributed to the anger of the ancestors nearly all are in connection with failure to fulfil marriage obligations. For this reason I am going to give a rather detailed account of the animals killed for wedding purposes, in order to establish the

---

baby is taken by its mother to her home for this occasion, the following children have their *imbeleko* offered only by their own descent group. All the other sacrifices listed above are offered to the patrilineal ancestors by their own descendants.

degree of their importance and also to distinguish those killed for sacrifices and those killed as a form of gift exchange. This is the account
of animals killed at a traditional wedding I witnessed on the 15th May,
1971.[1]

The progress of marriage arrangements is marked by sacrifices and
exchange of gifts. And each sacrifice or gift takes the arrangements a
step forward. I shall concern myself only with animals killed as sacrifices
or as gifts, and not with the other forms of gifts.

a. The bride's father at his home killed a goat "to accept the
negotiator of marriage" (*eyokuvuma umkhongi*). His brother sprinkled
the gall on the negotiator's right-hand index finger.

b. On a later occasion, the negotiator with a party from the groom's
people brought a variety of gifts for the bride's people. The bulk
of the gifts (*izibizo* from *biza*, vb., to name or to call for. In this
context the bride's mother lists or names the presents or gifts she
wants for herself) were for the bride's mother. On this occasion the
bride's father slaughtered a goat to honour the groom's mother. Such
a goat is referred to as *uhudo* (*huda*, vb., to suffer from diarrhoea),
because of the nursing care the woman gave to her son, the groom, as
a baby.

The negotiator presented the bride's mother with the *ubikibiki* goat
(*bikibiki* is anything of shaky and quivering nature such as jelly). It
signifies the "shaky and quivering" state of the woman's stomach
after giving birth to her child.

The negotiator's wife on the same occasion also presented a goat to
the bride, to signify that she should dress up her hair in the special
style (*inkehli*) worn by married women.

The bride in turn presented a goat to the negotiator's wife, in
appreciation of the latter's gift to her, which marked her new status.

All the goats exchanged on this day were slaughtered and eaten.
The groom's people took a portion of their meat back home.

c. Later on[2] the bride and her age-mates took food gifts (*umbondo*) to
the groom's home. Two goats known as *indlakudla* were slaughtered—
one for the bride and the other for her companion. The goats enabled
both the bride and her bridesmaid[3] to eat the food of the groom's

---

[1] The marriage negotiations had been going on for seven years before this wedding took place.
[2] After the harvest of the following year.
[3] The bridesmaid is a girl in her early teens, usually related to the bride. She remains with
the bride in her new home for some weeks after the marriage.

people, which was otherwise taboo to them. The gall of the two goats was sprinkled on the index finger of the bride's companion.

d. On a later occasion the groom paid a special ceremonial visit in the company of his age-mates and girls of his locality. A goat was slaughtered to enable him to eat the food of the bride's home. The gall was sprinkled on the negotiator. The goat is known as *indlakudla*.

e. At some other occasion the bride's father performed a nubility ceremony for her. He killed an ox and a goat, as well as another goat from her mother's brother. The gall of the three animals was sprinkled on her, and the gall bladders were inflated and worn on the head by her during the ceremony. When the ceremony was over the inflated bladders were carefully kept to be worn again on her wedding day. The gall bladder of the ox was pierced and worn by her as a wristlet. The ceremony is known as *ukwemula*.

f. A few days before the wedding the bride's father and his brothers went to the groom's home to "see" the *lobolo* cattle before they were transferred to the bride's home. The groom's father slaughtered a goat for the bride's father. The gall was sprinkled on her father's brother. The goat is known as *ilongwe*, i.e. the dry cake of cattle dung.

g. On the eve of the bride's leaving home to be married, her father slaughtered a goat known as *eyokuncama*. (*Ncama*, vb., to eat before commencing a long journey). This goat was intended to report her departure to the ancestors, and also to provide her with something to eat during her wedding ceremonies, as she was not supposed to eat any of the meat slaughtered on that occasion.

h. When the bridal party arrived, the groom's people gave them a goat called *eyokucola*. (*Ukucola* means "to give a feast in honour of the bride".) The gall was sprinkled on her companion, who also wore on her head the inflated bladder.

i. On the first day of the wedding a cow was presented by the groom to the bridal party. It is known as *eyesihlahla*, "the beast of the trees", because during the early part of the day the party sat outside the home under a tree where they cooked and ate the meat.

j. On the second day a cow provided by the bride's father to the groom's mother was slaughtered. The beast is known as *eyezibhoma*, which merely means "chunks" of meat.

k. On the same day the bride's people killed a goat and placed it in a large basin after piercing it to remove the gall, which was sprinkled on her by her father. She carried it unskinned and unopened in the basin, and presented it to her mother-in-law. The latter removed the basin from the bride's head and in return gave her a string of white beads. This action is known as *isethulo*, "to pay tribute, to make a present of respect". The carcase of such a goat is known as *isinyikan-yika*, translated by Doke and Vilakazi as "complicated affair, matter difficult of solution, something requiring disentangling."

l. The most important beast of all was also killed on the second day. It was a cow known sometimes as *eyesikhumba*, "the beast of the skin", as its skin is used to make a skirt for the bride. Another, more appropriate, name is *eyokwendisa* (*-enda*, vb., to undertake a long journey), since when a woman marries she is said to *ukwenda*, "to go on a long journey". This beast was—as is the custom—provided by the bride's father. It was slaughtered in the groom's cattle byre by the negotiator, who used a special ancestral spear belonging to the groom's people. (He himself was the groom's mother's brother.) The groom's mother sprinkled the gall on the bride's index finger and big toe, and herself wore the pierced and empty gall bladder as a wristlet. There are several other rituals surrounding this beast, which I cannot recount here. The carcase is bisected, and one half is given to the groom's people, the other being retained by the bride's. It is this beast that is said to "render the woman married".

m. Later in the day, i.e. on the second day, the bride's father went to the negotiator's home, where the groom's father had provided a goat known as *uthuli lomkhongi*, "the dust of the negotiator" (because during the period of negotiations he walked to and fro, between the two families). This goat is said to thank both the negotiator and the bride's father for bringing the negotiations to a happy conclusion.

n. On the third day, only the bride's age-mates remained. They were given a goat to kill, skin, cook, and eat to mark the consummation of the marriage. The goat is known as *umeke*, to split open, i.e. to deflower.

Table 1 shows more clearly how these exchanges of animal gifts and sacrifices are balanced.

I have mentioned the animals slaughtered in connection with this particular wedding. There may be differences elsewhere, but most of the Nyuswa people thought this wedding illustrated almost the whole range of Zulu wedding rites.

The purpose of listing here the animals killed for the wedding is to demonstrate that they are not always killed for purposes of sacrifice.

The basic criterion is the gall. It is significant that only the gall of sacrificial animals from the bride's people was sprinkled on her. (These are numbers 5, 6, 9, 10 in Table 1. In other cases where the gall features, such as numbers 1, 4, 8, it is sprinkled on people who represent a particular group. In each case the animal is provided by one group and the gall is sprinkled on a member of the other. The first group (i.e. the providers of the animal) sprinkle the second group (i.e. the receivers of the animal) with the gall, in order to introduce them to the provider's ancestors. The animals in numbers 2, 3, 7, 11 and 12 are not sacrifices, but just gifts, in which the gall does not feature.

These differences are important for the understanding of changes in the traditional wedding rites. In less elaborate wedding rituals, the animals slaughtered as gifts are fewer in number, and they tend to be converted into currency. This is understandable, because the gifts are subject to exchange. If the first party has not given a gift to start with, the second one has nothing to reciprocate. A good example of this is number 7, the ox, which is a present from the groom to the bridal party, and the cow, which is a present from the bride's father to the groom's mother. In this case, the initiator of the gift is the bride's father, who must indicate the beast that he is presenting. If the groom's family cannot afford a special beast to be given to the bridal party, his mother passes on to him her gift from the bride's father; he then gives it to the bridal party. In other words, for the bridal party to receive this particular gift from the groom the bride's father must have given it first.

Sacrifices given by one group for the other are easily converted to money instead of a slaughtered animal—provided that the recipients are prepared to accept the money. But where the sacrifice is for a member of the group, giving money would be tantamount to giving it to oneself. So, if people are unable to provide the necessary sacrifice, they offer incense to the ancestors, tell them the reasons for omitting the sacrifice, and express willingness to put the matter right at some future time.

Vilakazi has this to say:

> Throughout the negotiations, these gifts are anticipated because they are institutionalized, and each gift or goat begets another gift or goat. It is not uncommon to find that one of the parties requests that certain gifts should be cut out altogether. The request is often granted because in any case none of the gifts are unilateral.[1]
>
> 1962, p. 65

[1] On gifts see also Reader (1966, p. 207).

TABLE 1. The balancing of beasts given for slaughter

Beasts given by the bride's family	Gift or sacrifice	Purpose of slaughter
KILLED DURING THE PERIOD OF NEGOTIATIONS		
1. *Imvuma* goat killed for the negotiator on his second visit to the bride's home	Sacrifice	To report to the ancestors of the bride the beginning of marriage negotiations and point out the future affinal relationship represented by the negotiator
2. *Uhudo* goat slaughtered for the groom's mother on her ceremonial visit to the bride's home	Gift	A recognition and appreciation of her period of nursing and bringing up the groom
3. A goat slaughtered for the negotiator's wife who visits the bride's home on the same occasion as in (2) above	Gift	To thank her for her gift of a goat to the bride
4. *Indlakudla* goat for the groom on the occasion of his ceremonial visit to the bride's home	Sacrifice	To enable the groom to eat the food (excepting milk) at the bride's home and also to point him out to the bride's ancestors
5. *Ukwemula* ox and goat slaughtered for the bride at her own home	Sacrifice	The nubility beasts calculated to persuade the ancestors to make the bride reproductive
KILLED DURING THE WEDDING AS PART OF THE CEREMONY		
6. *Umncamo* goat for the bride on the eve of her departure	Sacrifice	To report to the ancestors her departure from her home to that of the affines
7. *Eyezibhoma* cow from the bride's father to the groom's mother, slaughtered at the groom's home during the wedding ceremony	Gift	To honour the groom's mother
8.		
9. *Eyesikhumba* ox. The most important beast surrounded by numerous rituals	Sacrifice	To surrender the bride to her affines, unite the two lineages in affinal relationship
10. *Isinyikanyika* goat given by the bride to her mother-in-law	Sacrifice	To pay respects to the mother-in-law and surrender herself to her as an understudy
11.		
12.		

by the two groups in marriage presentations and sacrifice

Beasts given by the groom's family	Gift or sacrifice	Purpose of slaughter
1. *Ilongwe* goat slaughtered for the bride's father when a few days before the wedding he visits the groom's home to "see" the *lobolo* cattle	Sacrifice	To report to the groom's ancestors the transference of the *lobolo* cattle and also to point out the bride's father who represents the new affinal relationship
2. *Ubikibiki* goat brought by the groom's people as part of the gifts to the bride's mother (*izibizo*)	Gift	An appreciation of her period of nursing and bringing up the bride
3. *Eyokukhehla* goat given by the negotiator's wife to the bride	Gift	The goat indicates that the bride should dress up her hair in a special way appropriate to married women
4. Two *indlakudla* goats for the bride and her companion on the occasion of their visit to present food gifts to the groom's house (*umbondo*)	Sacrifice	To enable the bride and her companion to eat the food
5.		
6.		
7. *Eyesihlahla* ox given by the groom to the bridal party slaughtered at the groom's home on the first day of the wedding	Gift	To honour the bridal party
8. *Eyekucola* goat slaughtered for the bride and given by the groom	Sacrifice	To welcome the bride and report her arrival to the ancestors. It was the first beast killed on the arrival of the bridal party
9.		
10.		
11. *Uthuli* goat given by the groom's father to the negotiator and the bride's father and slaughtered at the negotiator's home	Gift	To thank both the negotiator and the bride's father for having carried out negotiations which successfully led to marriage
12. *Umeke* goat from the groom to the bride's age-mates after the marriage has been consummated	Gift	To mark the end of the bride's virginity and her separation from her age-mates

It may seem peculiar that the elaborate wedding rituals seem to be primarily concerned with the bride and her mother-in-law. The wedding beast is sacrificed to integrate the bride into the lineage. The mother-in-law wears the gall bladder as a wristlet. Also, she receives the unique tribute of the unopened carcase of a goat. This becomes more understandable if we examine the meaning of the word *enda* used for marriage in Zulu. Literally, it means "to go on a long journey", the journey in this case being the transference of the bride from her home to the groom's home. The main beast "weds" her (*eyamendisa*) and links her with her groom's people. The link is symbolized by the gall that is sprinkled on her and the gall bladder worn by her mother-in-law. Since it is the bride who is transferred and who is expected to be fertile, it is not surprising that she is surrounded by many rituals to effect her transfer and her fertility at a mystical level. The groom is said to "take her" (*uyathatha*), whereas she "travels" to him (*uyenda*).

The bride and her mother-in-law are the two people who have "travelled a long journey" to perpetuate the lineage of their affines. The bride has come to continue where the mother-in-law had stopped; she has come to further the reproduction. The *isinyikaryika* goat, which the bride presents to her mother-in-law, suggests that she is giving herself as an understudy to the latter, who will orientate her in the routine and practices of the family.

I must also mention here that a married woman has the status more of a mother than a wife. In English culture, for instance, if Miss Jones marries Mr. Smith, she becomes Mrs Smith, his wife. In Zulu culture she would become "Mother Jones" (Ma Jones). She retains her clan name, and in this sense she is someone who has come to her affinal lineage to be a mother. It is therefore not surprising that marriage rites are focused on the bride and her mother-in-law. They are the mothers of the lineage, on whom the continuity of the lineage is dependent.

Further implications of motherhood will appear in Chapter 6, where I examine the relationship between motherhood and pollution.

Meanwhile I must mention that marriage rituals with regard to their emphasis on motherhood can bring about social maternity.

A good instance is provided by the case of a man who had two wives. The first wife had three girls only, and the second had a boy and a girl. When the son of the second wife got married he used the *lobolo* cattle of the first wife's daughters, on the understanding that his bride would be placed into the house of the first wife to perpetuate it (*avuse indlu*, to raise the house), as she had no boys. Although the family was by now Lutheran, the son married according to traditional Zulu custom (i.e. not according to Christian marriage), in order to be free to take a second wife and place her in his own mother's house. His bride performed all the wedding rites in relation to the first wife as her mother-in-law. She later had seven children, three of whom are boys. Her husband had married three other women, who all belonged to the house of the second wife (his biological mother). But none of them bore him any children. His father and his two "mothers" are now dead, and he is the head of the homestead. Whenever he sacrifices for the benefit of his children (for instance, performs an *imbeleko* sacrifice), he calls upon his father and his father's senior wife to protect them, since they belong to her through the marriage rites. But when he sacrifices for his own benefit he calls upon his father and his own mother (his father's second wife). The problem now facing the family is that his own mother's house will not be perpetuated, since none of the three women belonging to it have children. This could be solved if the eldest son of his first wife, who is already married, would marry another woman and place her in the house of the second wife. Alternatively, a younger son could marry and place his wife in that house. But the mother of these sons does not get on well with her co-wives, and she refuses to accede to this suggestion, which cannot be adopted without her consent.

This case is a good illustration of the meaning behind the rites surrounding a bride and her mother-in-law.

I have dwelt on the ritual of marriage to emphasize the point that the illnesses and misfortunes believed to be caused by ancestral wrath are mainly associated with the non-fulfilment of marriage obligations. The following figures are indicative of this.

Information was collected on the married couples within one hundred homesteads. I am interested here in sacrifice, particularly the one believed to make the woman wedded, i.e. "the ox of the skin" (*eyesikhumba*, No. 9 in Table 1). There were 258 married women. Of these, 166 (63 per cent) had had the "ox of the skin" sacrifice, 45 (18 per cent) had only a goat slaughtered by the groom's people on arrival (to report the circumstances and a hope of having a wedding ceremony some time in the future), and 47 (19 per cent) had had no sacrifice at all. Except for 5 cases in the last category, all the women had had marriage negotiations started and some marriage exchanges made. In almost all cases where there was no sacrifice or where only a goat was sacrificed, marriage negotiations had dragged on for a long time (3 to 10 years); the woman got pregnant, and on taking the baby to the groom's people for its first sacrifice (*imbeleko*) she usually stayed on and never returned home. Some women claimed that they had come only temporarily to bring the baby for an *imbeleko* sacrifice or because it was ill, that they would return home as soon as possible. It was difficult to discriminate between those who would return home and those who would remain permanently, particularly because the history of most unions where no sacrifice was performed, or ultimately one of a goat, started in this way. This group consisted mainly of younger women, at most in their early thirties. They included cases such as that of case 3 (see p. 49), as well as some in which a woman's father wanted all the *lobolo* paid before he would consider letting her get married, or in which the father had died and the heir was unwilling to shoulder the wedding expenses. Without exception, such women regarded themselves as not properly married, even in cases where the marriage had been registered at the magistrate's court.

The kind of misfortune usually suffered by women for whom no sacrifice at all had been performed to report their presence was attributed to the husband's ancestors wanting to know "who they were" by making their children ill, or else such women experienced "heaviness" at night and heard voices saying: "Who are you? What do you want here?" Those who had only goats slaughtered to report their presence within the homestead tended to experience misfortunes of "no peace" in the family (i.e. quarrelling over trivial matters between spouses). Their children were also sickly. Properly wedded women suffered such misfortunes as sterility, miscarriage, or delayed conception owing to non-fulfilment either of nubility rites or gift exchange on the wedding day or anger of the woman's ancestors because *lobolo* cattle were still owing.

Associated with the ancestral anger, 11 cases of death, 14 of illness and 19 of other misfortunes were reported (see Chapter 7).

Of the deaths, 9 were of children deprived of ancestral protection owing to non-fulfilment of marriage duties. The other 2 were due to the anger of ancestors owing to neglect of other duties (cf, case 1, p. 48).

The illnesses included 3 cases of women who experienced sleeplessness at night because of "heaviness in the house" and voices whispering into their ears and asking who they were. In 7 cases children became ill, either because the ancestors wanted to know who their mothers were or because they were dissatisfied with the delay of marriage rites. The

4 other cases were attributed to non-fulfilment of duties unconnected with marriage rites; for instance, a woman kept quarrelling with her mother-in-law, and as a result her children became ill.

The 19 miscellaneous cases of misfortune included 4 of sterility, 2 of delayed conception, 2 of children being either few in number or all of the female sex, 6 of discord between spouses, and 5 of desertion by one of the spouses.

Although these figures merely reflect tendencies, I believe they justify the attention I have given in this chapter to marriage sacrifices, as they indicate the main cause of ancestral anger.

However, I must mention here that in reply to the question: "What type of actions annoy the ancestors most?" (*Yiziphi izenzo ezibacasula kakhulu abaphansi?*), the answer was usually: "Quarrelling within the homestead" (*umsindo ekhaya*, the noise within the home). Yet according to the cases ancestral anger is most often aroused by non-fulfilment of marriage duties. If anything, lack of "peace in the home" is, in the cases reported, an indication rather than the cause, of misfortunes owing to anger of the ancestors. I believe the answer to the question above was often an abstraction based on the assumption that the marriage duties and other duties towards the ancestors should have been performed.

I want now to comment on some sociological interpretations of ancestral behaviour, more particularly the analysis suggested by J. D. McKnight.

McKnight has written an interesting paper on "Extra-Descent Group Cults in African Societies" (*Africa*, 1967, pp. 1–21). In it he questions Radcliffe-Brown's observation: "The father punishes his children, and so may the ancestors on the father's side. On the other hand, the mother is tender and indulgent to her child, and her relatives are expected to be the same, and so also the maternal spirits." (1952, p. 28.) In other words, in patrilineal societies the maternal ancestors are believed to be benevolent because the maternal relatives, who are without jural authority, are benevolent.

McKnight, in questioning this "extension" theory, cites the LoDagaba situation as described by Goody and the Tallensi as described by Fortes. Among the LoDagaba the relationship with the mother's brother is often one of considerable conflict, yet the mother's brother's spirit is not aggressive (Goody, 1962, pp. 20, 282, 430). Fortes (1959, p. 235) writes: "But the spirits of female ancestors are believed to be specially hard, cruel and capricious. This is remarkable when we consider the love and devotion a mother shows her child throughout his life." McKnight further argues that in most patrilineal societies (such as the Tsonga, Bhaca and Mpondo of Southern Africa) the maternal ancestors may be regarded as a cause of misfortune. He then proceeds to demonstrate that among matrilineal societies the extra-descent ancestors (i.e. the paternal ancestors) may also be a cause of illness, although they have no jural responsibility over their descendants.

He points out that the infant is both kin through blood ties to his extra-descent group and also an affinal relative when he represents his descent group.

He concludes by observing that it is in the role of an affinal relationship that the extra-descent group ancestors make the infant ill. They use him to bargain for their rights in the affinal relationship, as he is the only one they can reach in his descent group. He writes:

> It is therefore not surprising that the sister's son may be used as a vehicle of revenge by the bride wealth-receiving groups to enforce their rights. . . . If we view the power attributed to the extra-descent group ancestors as a means of enforcing rights over members of an affinally related descent group, then, to some degree, the punitive aspect of the extra-descent group ancestors becomes understandable.
>
> 1967, pp. 16–17

In support of this view, he cites Middleton who, on the Lugbara, has this to say:

> The hostility felt by the mother's brother's group against the sister's son is directed against him not as a sister's son, a relative by "blood", but as a representative of the potentially hostile affinal lineage. He is the victim merely because being connected by "blood" it is only he who is liable to be affected in this way.
>
> 1960, p. 57

In Table 1 it is indicated how the bride's father has to provide a number of sacrificial animals which are intended to render the bride fertile. By these sacrifices he guarantees her fertility. Should he omit them he is likely to be responsible if his daughter does not conceive, or miscarries, or if her babies die or sicken. In such a case it is his ancestors who interfere with her fertility because the relevant rites that would enable them to promote it have not been performed.

Case 2 (p. 48) demonstrates this. MaDladla, whose nubility rites (*ukwemula*) had not been performed, could not conceive, because of the "heavy presence" of the spirits of her ancestors at her affinal home.

Annoyed over the omission of the nubility rites, they had accompanied her there. To correct this they had to be fetched by her father, who later invited her back home to perform her belated nubility rites. In this case the ancestors were angry with her father, their own descendant, for failing to fulfil his duties.

Reader says of the Makhanya-Zulu:

> An important part of the wedding preparations by the girl's group at this stage is the assembly of these cattle. The *ukwendisa* (giving in marriage) consist essentially of two beasts: the *inkabi yezinkomo*, an ox sometimes known as the *impandla kayise* (father's bald head), a thank-offering to the father of the boy for the *lobolo* cattle, and the *isikhumba*, a beast nominally to make the bride a skirt, but in reality having a ritual significance in joining the ancestors of the two descent groups. . . . The beasts bear the ancestral sanction that if they are not provided the bride will eventually fail or miscarry in childbirth. . . .
>
> 1966, p. 194

Although Reader does not tell us which ancestors are particularly annoyed by the omission, he does confirm that the girl's father has to provide the cattle which are sacrificed to promote her reproductivity.

However, the woman's ancestors can only be expected to promote her fertility if the husband's people have fulfilled their part of the marriage obligations in terms of *lobolo* and other exchanges. If such exchanges are omitted the maternal ancestors may interfere with the conception or make the baby ill as an expression of their anger against the affinal relations.

It is not only the maternal ancestors who may express their displeasure in this way. The paternal ancestors also disapprove if marriage obligations towards them or towards their descendants have not been fulfilled.

Case 3 (p. 49) is a good example of ancestors being annoyed by non-fulfilment of the obligations by their own descendants towards them. Because they had not been requested to protect the womb from which the baby came, they declined to protect the baby when requested to do so, as they considered this as putting the cart before the horse.

Vilakazi gives another example of a case where paternal ancestors were angry with their affinal relations. He writes:

> A case of failure to give the requisite gifts which resulted in illness was quoted from a Goba family among the Qadi. The *umakoti* (bride) did not give any *umabo* gifts to the deceased grandfather of the boy. A younger "father" drew the attention of the lineage to this omission, but he was told that since the family was Christian, they were not going to give to the dead as that would constitute worshipping ancestral spirits.

A few days after marriage, however, the *umakoti* fell ill and, as she was already pregnant, miscarried. This was explained by the old people as being due to the anger of the gods and the girl's father was asked to provide a beast to appease the ancestral spirits, which was done.

1962, pp. 68–69

This suggests that ancestral wrath over marriage obligations can be reduced to four variables:

a. When the woman's ancestors are annoyed by their own descendants.
b. When her ancestors are annoyed by her husband's people.
c. When the husband's ancestors are angry with their own descendants.
d. When his ancestors are angry with his wife's people.

To appreciate the variables let us remind ourselves that the expectation is that a man will marry during his parents' lifetime. If the proper marriage observances are not performed, the ancestors may, for instance, hold responsible the groom's father, whose duty it is to see to those obligations. The crucial point here is that such ancestors are in fact the baby's father's father's and partly its father's effective ancestors. When the baby reaches manhood and sacrifices in his own right, he will be sacrificing to his father and his father's father. This means that the ancestors who protect the baby do so on behalf of its grandfather and father, as these are the people who stand to lose if there are no progeny to sacrifice to them. Thus, if the ancestors allow the baby to become ill, they could well be threatening to cut off the progeny of its grandfather and father, as they themselves would not lose anything by that. They may well use this as pressure to get recognition and appreciation of their protection. In the case of the twins mentioned above, the diviner harped on the fact that the ancestors wanted to know who was the mother of the twins, which in fact is another way of saying: "You cannot take us for granted and expect us to protect the womb from which the seed germinates."

The question that arises is: To what extent can the descent interpretation hold true for maternal ancestors?

To be childless is considered a great affliction by a married woman and her own people. She cannot form a uterine (*kwethu*) unit that constitutes an economic unit and assures her of a comfortable middle or old age when her daughter-in-law takes care of her. Child-bearing also ensures the perpetuation of her name as an ancestress of her own sons and grandsons. It is therefore in the interest of her people that she gets children who grow up to maturity, as this would not only make her later life comfortable, but in the life hereafter she would be an ancestress.

The descent principle can thus explain all four variables of ancestral anger over marriage obligations: it is in the interest of the living to satisfy the ancestors by fulfilling the marriage obligations, as this ensures that the ancestors will protect the issue of the marriage, who in turn will perpetuate the names of the living generations as ancestors.

This may seem to suggest that female children have no place in the descent scheme; since descent is from male to male, female children would not be used as a lever to exert pressure. In answer to this it must be noted that girls make it possible to "raise the house", since *lobolo* accruing from a daughter's marriage may enable an agnatic relation to marry a woman to perpetuate a descent line which has no male issue.

The expectation is that one dies in old age, leaving married sons who perform rituals that integrate the spirit with the body of ancestors and enable it to come home and operate as an ancestor or ancestress. This is the type of "heaven" in the context of ancestral cult. Any spirit which is not integrated with the others wanders about and leads a lonely and miserable life. It is in some sort of "limbo" or hell for the spirit and this is the most undesirable situation.

McKnight has also used the descent principle to explain the extra-descent ancestor cult behaviour and sees it as a means of pressurizing the affinal group to fulfil their obligations. This approach does not adequately explain the four variables. It cannot, for instance, be used to explain the cases where maternal ancestors among the Zulu interfere with fertility to register their disapproval of their own descendants.

We can now examine McKnight's main thesis that, contrary to Radcliffe-Brown's extension principle, maternal ancestors are not as benevolent as living maternal relations, in that such ancestors may be regarded as a cause of illness.

While the Zulu material confirms McKnight's observation that maternal ancestors sometimes do cause illness, it does not necessarily validate the rejection of Radcliffe-Brown's assertion. Among the Zulu, all things being equal (e.g. marriage obligations duly fulfilled), maternal ancestors would have no reason to interfere with fertility. In general, people try hard to fulfil the marriage obligations, and the expectation is that the obligations will be fulfilled, or an agreement is reached that will satisfy both groups. "Malevolent" behaviour by maternal ancestors is an exception rather than a rule. Accordingly, it may well be said that these ancestors are benevolent save in exceptional cases.

This is confirmed by Wilson's material on the Nyakyusa (1957, p. 181). McKnight quotes her as saying:

> In all the cases we traced, in which a woman's ancestors were believed to have made her, or her child, ill, there was a dispute between her father (or his heir) and her husband over marriage cattle or the bull of puberty; and we were told that her father's shades are angry only if marriage cattle have not been paid and for no other reason.

In pointing out that the Zulu material does not necessarily invalidate Radcliffe-Brown's theory, I do not claim that he had that material in mind when he made the statements related to maternal ancestors. For instance, he writes:

> But though, according to the statements made to me, the maternal ancestors will not punish their descendant with sickness, they can be appealed to for help. When, therefore, a child is sick the parents may go to the mother's brother of the child, or to the mother's father if he is still living, and ask that a sacrifice shall be offered, and an appeal for help made to the child's maternal ancestors. This, at any rate, is stated as a practice in the Sotho tribes, and one of the purposes of the *ditsoa* cattle that go from the marriage payment to the mother's brother of the bride is said to be to make provision for such sacrifices if they should be needed.
>
> 1952, p. 27

I find the last sentence somewhat confusing in that the recipient of the *ditsoa* cattle is the child's mother's mother's brother, not its own mother's brother.

The passage above gives the impression that Radcliffe-Brown was not aware of the fact that maternal ancestors are sometimes believed to cause illness. McKnight thus had reason to question the assertion that "the maternal ancestors will not punish their descendants with sickness". The greatest weakness of Radcliffe-Brown's extension theory is that he bases his argument on emotional sentiment—which cannot be measured. In addition, I believe, it is open to question whether in causing the illness the maternal ancestors are really malevolent against the baby. The living maternal relations are benevolent on a person-to-person basis, between mother's father and daughter's children, or between mother's brother and sister's children. In cases of any maternal ancestral anger over the marriage obligations, that anger is directed against the baby's father's father (or its father), whose responsibility it is to fulfil the marriage obligations. The relationship of dispute is between the maternal ancestors and the baby's paternal grandfather, and the dispute is whether such a grandfather is entitled to have a grandchild. I would therefore argue that the children are the centre of dispute, and the question of benevolence or malevolence towards them does not arise.

There is yet another point which must be considered in an analysis of this kind. This is the importance of the time factor in the development cycle.

If all the marriage obligations have been fulfilled, the maternal ancestors are not expected to interfere with the reproductivity. This suggests that their displeasure can be related to a definite time in that they signal their displeasure during the early stages of marriage. Once whatever annoys them is put right, subsequent illness of the children would be attributed to something else.

If we take into account the time factor we can more readily understand how the relationship of the individual to the ancestors changes during the different stages of his life.

I have already mentioned how the maternal ancestors are interested in the baby as evidence of their daughter's fertility, which they had guaranteed on marriage. They extend a tacit protection over the baby even though they have no jural powers over it. As it grows into an adult its mother becomes more and more identified with her affines, and when she dies her spirit is integrated with the spirits of her affines, not with those of her own people. She becomes a "patrilineal" rather than a maternal ancestor in that she is identified with the patrilineal ancestors of her children.

I make this point here to draw attention to the possible differences in permutations of the ancestral structure in patrilineal societies.

For instance, the Zulu and the Tallensi are in sharp contrast with regard to maternal ancestorship. On the Tallensi, Fortes has this to say:

> Nevertheless it is a basic assumption that a wife never ceases entirely to be a "stranger" in her husband's clan. For she never, as we have learnt, loses the social identity conferred on her by birth as a member of a different clan. She does not adopt her husband's totemic taboos, and though her health and fertility, being essential for the satisfactory performance of her wifely role, come under the guardianship of his ancestors, she does not participate in the cult of his lineage ancestors.
>
> 1949, pp. 98–99

It is important to consider notional differences in different patrilineal societies when discussing maternal ancestors. In the case of the
Zulu, for instance, one cannot discuss fruitfully the role of the maternal
ancestors without establishing the point in time one is concerned with
in a particular context.

In concluding this chapter I want to point out that perhaps one of the
most important points it has revealed is the dilemma that faces married
women in a society with strong patrilineal leanings such as that of the
Zulu. Exogamy rules are very stringent, in that a man avoids marrying
not only women of his own clan, but all who belong to his mother's clan,
or to a grandmother's clan (on either side), or even a great grandmother's clan, or who have relationship with any of these clans. So the
women that are married are strangers, upon whose fecundity the husband is dependent for the perpetuation of his descent group. Given the
system of belief that a wife's fertility is essentially dependent on the
fulfilment of marriage obligations by both parties (i.e. her family and
her husband's), she depends entirely on the sense of responsibility of
these two groups. She may miscarry, fail to conceive, or have chronically
sick children, as a result of ancestral wrath over unfulfilled marriage
duties; but she is helpless, as she cannot in her own right appease the
ancestors or correct what is wrong.

What is further ironical is that even when marriage duties have been
duly fulfilled, her motherhood (reproductive period) makes her an outsider, hemmed in on all sides by various rules of over respect and
avoidance (*ukuhlonipha*) from which she is only released by menopause.
It is this logic that determines her roles as a mother and wife, a daughter
and sister, which I want to examine in the next chapter, as I believe
that it will throw further light on the conflicting interests in the rules
of patriliny and exogamy.

5 | Pollution

Because, among the Zulu, "pollution" is a "mystical force" more often closely associated with women, in this chapter I shall look at the position of women and their interaction with mystical forces in their roles as daughters, mothers and wives.

Among Zulu the source of pollution is essentially a happening associated with "birth" on the one hand and "death" on the other. Both birth and death are mysteries associated with the other world from which people are believed to come and to which people return in spirit form. Although "this world" and the "other world" are viewed as two separate entities, the beginning of life, whose source is believed to be in the "other world", happens in "this world", and the cessation of life in "this world" is believed to mean continuity of life in the "other world". Notionally there is an area of overlap between the two worlds. Such an area is marginal and dangerous.[1] Professor Edmund Leach has this to say on such marginality:

> The physical and temporal environment in which man exists is a continuum, but we perceive it as made of discontinuous elements. We do this by making arbitrary discriminations of value between the different sections of the continua. Taboo is part of this discriminating process. If two adjacent sections of a continuum are recognized as discrete and separate, then that section of the continuum which is marginal and adjacent to both discriminate sections becomes the object of inhibition and taboo.
>
> 1971, p. 24

Thus among Zulu the overlap believed to exist between "this world" and the "other world" is expressed by the term *umnyama*, which literally means "darkness". In later chapters we shall note how the darkness of

[1] See also Douglas, M. (1966).

the night is symbolically seen as representing death, while the daylight represents life. *Umnyama*, when used metaphorically to symbolize death, can be translated as "pollution". Pollution, then, is viewed as a marginal state between life and death.

Umnyama (pollution) is conceptualized as a mystical force which diminishes resistance to disease, and creates conditions of poor luck, misfortune (*amashwa*), "disagreeableness" and "repulsiveness" (*isidina*) whereby the people around the patient take a dislike to him without any provocation. In its worst form *umnyama* is contagious.

The behaviour pattern observed by those in a state of *umnyama* is known as *ukuzila*. It entails withdrawal from social life, abstinence from all pleasurable experiences, avoidance of quarrelling and fighting, and avoidance of wearing any finery. People are expected to speak in low tones and only when necessary. They also either fast or eat only small quantities of sloppy food. Since *umnyama* is graded according to its intensity, the extent of *ukuzila* is dependent on the intensity of the particular phase of *umnyama*. Because polluted people are said to be accident prone and vulnerable to all sorts of misfortune, they avoid all risky and dangerous undertakings, such as firing pottery, which depends on luck, or swimming, which is dangerous.

Of the *umnyama* that arises from reproductive situations, the most highly intensified point is associated with a newly delivered mother (*umdlezane*). She is dangerous to herself, to her baby and particularly to males, who not only become vulnerable because of her pollution but whose virility also suffers if they eat food cooked by her or share eating utensils with her. During the first three days she must not leave the house at all. Even her husband may not come into the hut where she is confined until the cord drops off from the baby. After three days, whenever she goes out she covers herself with a blanket. After ten days the hut is cleaned out and the floor freshly smeared with cow-dung. She may then go out of the house without a blanket. But this does not mean the end of her pollution. As long as she still has the afterbirth emission she is dangerous. She avoids mixing with people and no man would dare to share eating utensils with her. If she must go to the shops, or to gather firewood, or fetch water from the river, she smears red ochre on the exposed parts of her body to protect herself from the dangers to which she is exposed.

She must also avoid cattle, cattle byres and all milk food, as her contamination is believed to dry up the udders of the milking cows. She avoids going through fields, because the growing plants may shrivel up and wither away. Groundnuts (*izindlubu*) are the most sensitive.

The baby is endangered in the sense that the contamination which the mother easily contracts in the environment because of her polluted state of low resistance is passed on through her breasts. An *umdlezane* goes out of her home only if she must. On her return she squeezes her breasts to let the first portion of her milk drip on the floor or on the fireplace before feeding her baby. This is said to remove any contamination she might have contracted. She remains an *umdlezane* until the flow of after-birth emissions stops. Her contagion and danger particularly to men also stops. But she still remains with some form of *umnyama*, of reduced intensity, and this lasts as long as she is lactating. Her lactating period is comparable to her gestation period, when her vulnerability, though not contagious to other people, is nevertheless a threat to her baby. For this reason a lactating mother and a pregnant woman avoid contaminating situations such as contact with death. As a protective measure against unforeseen contamination, pregnant and nursing mothers often smear red ochre on the soles of their feet. The significance of red ochre will be clear when I deal with colour symbolism in relation to the treatment of disease.

A menstruating woman also has a contagious pollution which, however, is not considered as dangerous as that of a newly delivered mother (*umdlezane*). This is evidenced by the fact that she may mix with men. She becomes a danger to their virility only if she has sexual intercourse with them. She also avoids cattle and crops. If she must go through an *izindlubu* field, she spits on a sod of soil and throws it into the field before going into it herself. This is said to protect the plants from her pollution.

Men, as well as women, are considered polluted during the day following sexual intercourse. The pollution is of a milder form and is not contagious. Men abstain from sexual intercourse the night before undertaking such enterprises as hunting, sacrifice, and forging spears (in the case of iron smiths). It is said that in former times they also abstained on the night before setting out on a war campaign. We shall later see how such enterprises share a common factor.

Sexual intercourse is polluting not only because of the sex act but also because of the seminal emissions. Bryant writes:

> There were always a number of lads lacking sweethearts with whom to have intercourse. Should a youth be seen in the morning betaking himself to the river, it was thereby known that he was going there on account of an involuntary nocturnal emission. 1949, p. 573

The going to the river suggests a cleansing ritual, which indicates that seminal emission is polluting.

If seminal emission happens in sexual intercourse a cleansing ritual is not observed, except in cases where sexual intercourse is resumed after abstinence dating from the birth of the baby. The rite is known as "stepping over the baby" (ukweq' umntwana). It is calculated to protect the baby from the pollution associated with intercourse. After intercourse the mother washes her hands in water to which pounded tambootie grass roots (isiqunga) are added. The following morning the baby is given an enema with an infusion of tambootie roots. This is done once—on the first night of resumption of sexual intercourse. If it is not, it is said the baby will be weak and unattractive to people.

All the above instances (of different degrees of pollution) are associated with the manifestations of conditions of reproductivity, and the pollution is experienced by the person concerned.

There is, however, another reproductive situation which differs from those mentioned above in that it is not an individual, but a group, experience. This happens in the case of the unmarried girls who are organized in age-groups. If one of them becomes pregnant before marriage, this is considered a "bad precedent" which mystically endangers her age-mates. As soon as they realize that she is pregnant, they perform a ritual to rid themselves of the pollution. Pregnancy is supposed to happen within the context of marriage, and even then it is polluting, but if it happens before marriage its pollution takes on a new dimension. It is considered as having "opened the way for further misfortunes". It is a bad precedent which is likely to repeat itself. This is expressed by the term umkhokha (or umswazi). Hence, when the girls perform the cleansing rituals, they are said to remove umkhokha. Before cleansing rituals are carried out the girls can be regarded as "marginal" as they are said to be vulnerable and weakened by the wrongful act of one of their members.

I shall now consider pollution associated with death. This highly intensified form of pollution emanates from the corpse itself and from the chief mourner who is closely associated with the deceased. It is significant that the chief mourner is always a married woman. She is the chief mourner when her husband and her unmarried children die. In cases where the deceased's nearest relative is a man, it is nevertheless a woman who is the chief mourner. In English usage, for instance, if a woman whose sons are already married dies, her nearest relation is her husband, and therefore it is he who should be the chief mourner. But among the Zulu the daughter-in-law is the chief mourner for the dead woman. If a son's wife dies, the chief mourner is not himself but his mother, who mourns the death of her daughter-in-law. An unmarried woman is never a chief mourner. I shall return later to the significance of a woman as chief mourner.

The other bereaved persons are also polluted and their pollution is contagious, but the degree of intensity is less than that of the chief mourner.

Persons who actually handle the corpse, or help with the burial in any way, are considered more polluted than people who are merely present at the burial.

The cause of death is also an important factor in assessing the degrees of pollution. For instance, a catastrophic death has a special degree of intensity in that its pollution is said to cling to the bereaved in such a manner as to cause further disasters and calamities. Unfortunate happenings, such as death owing to an accident or because of an incurable disease, are regarded as an unusual misfortune expressed as *umkhokha*. The bereaved in these circumstances have to take precautions to ward off not only *umnyama* that arises from death, but also the special kind of *umnyama* that is *umkhokha*.

As a precautional measure against *umkhokha*, people who die in accidents such as a car crash or by drowning, or who are struck by lightning, or who die fighting, or who are murdered, are never brought within the home premises, but are buried outside without ceremony, while weeping is restrained. The same applies also to those who die of incurable diseases such as epilepsy and chronic chest diseases.

Taking a human life adds another dimension to the degree of pollution: in addition to the pollution that arises from death as from catastrophic death, the killer himself is polluted in a special way. His intention is not important. He may have killed in self-defence, accidentally, at war, or committed a cold-blooded murder. He may have killed a stranger or his kinsman. But he is polluted as lonn as he takes a human life.

Death is sometimes symbolically represented in the treatment of certain types of disease by administering "black" medicines. The relevance of this treatment here is that during the period when the patients are thus treated, they withdraw from society and behave like bereaved people (*ukuzila*). They are considered to be polluted during this period and their pollution is contagious.

We have so far noted that the contagious nature of pollution differs from one condition to the other. For instance, to be near a corpse by being present at the burial gives one a mild form of pollution, but to touch it inflicts a stronger form of pollution, which requires more elaborate cleansing rites.

We have also noted that not all forms of pollution are transferable. For instance, a pregnant or a nursing mother, though dangerous to her baby, is not dangerous to other people.

Fighting and sexual intercourse are considered effective means of transmitting transferable pollution to those who are not polluted. In other words, if one is hit by, or has sexual intercourse with, a bereaved person, this is pollution in a milder form, and it cannot be passed on to a third person. Such boundaries provide a control mechanism to protect the society from pollution of epidemic proportions.

Although pollution is a mystical force which shows no somatic symptoms, it is rather interesting that flouting of the correct behaviour (*ukuzila*) is said to result in some form of neurosis. This notion is expressed as *ukudlula* (-*dlula*, vb., to pass, to surpass). In the context of pollution, it means to become incorrigible in flouting social restraints and social expectations as if by involuntary compulsion. A person who because of her polluted state withdraws from society is expected among other things to be soft spoken, control her emotions, and avoid sexual intercourse; if she does not observe these rules she may become a sexual pervert, speak or sing when she should not, and be aggressive without any provocation. She is said to have no control over her actions, as she has *dlula*. In the case of a homicide this is expressed as *iqungo* (bloodlust) whereby such a person is over-aggressive and ready to kill other people.

What is significant here is that the sanctions are cast in psychological concepts. This suggests that the emotional stresses endured during both birth and death—the two mainsprings of pollution—are prevented from initiating neuroses by the diversion of focus from the unpleasant experience to a complexity of ritual behaviour. The mental stresses and strains experienced during the major life crises are seen as a possible cause of permanent damage to some people's mental balance, and this is expressed as an outcome of flouting the behaviour pattern.

To understand the meaning of pollution among the Zulu, it is necessary to look more closely into pollution at its highest points, i.e. birth and death.

I have no intention of giving details of mortuary rites, but I find it necessary to elaborate on the central role of the married woman who is designated as chief mourner.

As soon as a person dies, the corpse is prepared by the chief mourner (i.e. the eyes and mouth are shut, the body washed, and the limbs straightened). She is helped in this by other married women of the lineage. The burial usually takes place on the day after death. Throughout the intervening period, the chief mourner sits on the bare floor next to the corpse, covered up in a blanket. She fasts, and maintains silence. Only married women sit with her and the corpse. During the burial, she sits silently next to the grave covered up in a blanket. The blanket is removed from her face after the burial and only then may she speak. She, however, continues to be in mourning and must observe *ukuzila* (abstinence) behaviour until she is ritually released. This usually happens after three months if the deceased was a baby or child, six months if an unmarried adult and one year if her husband. The other members of the family are released much earlier from mourning. This also depends upon the status of the deceased. If he was a married man and a head of a homestead, the relatives are released by a hunting ritual (*ihlambo*, "the washing of spears") after three months or earlier. In the Nyuswa area ritual hunting is done by the deceased's male kinsmen. In one instance they could not find any wild animal or game to kill, so they killed two rats and a snake. These were brought home and placed at the main entrance into the homestead. The important thing, I was told, was that some wild animal must be killed and brought home.

The account given above is of a modern funeral where a coffin is used and the grave is not round. I did not have the opportunity of observing "truly" traditional mortuary rites where no coffin is used. This does not, however, mean that the traditional interment has completely died out. Some people in the Nyuswa area preferred it.

To appreciate the role of the chief mourner it is important to look into more traditional mortuary rites. For this I depend mainly on an account given by Bryant (1949, pp. 698–709).[1]

He tells us that while still supple the corpse was prepared by the wives (the deceased was their husband), who sat it up on its haunches and made it lean against the hindmost pillar of the central fireplace

---

[1] This account is a description of funerary rites for a married man because it is he who is considered a complete person. Women, children and unmarried men have less elaborate funerary rites.

facing the upper part of the hut. The knees were bent up and the arms bent back uncrossed with hands touching either side of the chin. The corpse was bound up to stiffen in this position and then it was covered with a skin blanket.

In the meanwhile the grave was dug just above the cattle-fold within the homestead by neighbours and brothers of the deceased, but not by his sons. The grave itself was a round pit, three or four feet deep, in the wall of which a niche had been excavated sufficiently large to receive a body.

The wives carried the corpse to the doorway of the hut, where it was received by men who conveyed it to the graveside and placed it down upon a mat beside the open grave. The principal wife cut off the dead man's head ring, washed the head, and removed the blanket and the cord that tied the corpse. After this she descended into the grave and received from the men above her husband's corpse, which she carefully placed within the niche, seated upon a mat of hide and rushes and facing towards the cattle-fold. Having placed the corpse, she joined her co-wives who were kneeling in a bowed posture near the grave in silent grief. The sons and daughters did not sit with their mothers.

On the following day, before dawn, the widows went to the river, where each washed her whole body and face, but not the head. With top knots dishevelled and leather kilts turned inside out, they returned home. There, on the grass outside the gate, they found many of the neighbouring women already assembled for the "wailing" ceremony. At such a ceremony every woman in the surrounding homesteads was duty bound to put in an appearance. With hands behind their heads, or wringing their hands, the women wailed until they were exhausted. This communal wailing (*isililo*) continued throughout the day as more and more women arrived. Finally, each party went to the river to sprinkle the whole body with water before going home.[1] Meanwhile an ox was slaughtered to cleanse the hands of those who had helped with the burial.

When the widow delivers a corpse to the lineage men at the doorway her action corresponds to delivering a baby to the lineage at birth.[2] The corpse is tied up in such a manner that it more or less represents a foetus in the womb—with its knees and arms bent up. The hut with the

[1] The wailing ceremony was omitted if the deceased had died of old age.
[2] This is my own interpretation which arises from association of rites and analogies of the hut and the womb, referred to later on.

corpse and mourners together within it symbolizes the confinement hut as well as the womb itself. (That the round hut is sometimes thought of as analogous to the womb was often brought home to me when respondents explained the relative seniority of twins. I was told that if two people enter a hut, the first to enter sits away from the doorway while the second sits nearer to it. So when they leave, it will be the one sitting nearer the doorway who will go out first. According to this logic the second twin is therefore senior.[1] Furthermore, uterine siblings are said to belong to the same hut, which is sometimes expressed as the womb—*abendlu yinye, abesisu sinye*, "They are of one hut, they are of one womb". It is because of such analogies that I see the handing of the corpse to the men as symbolizing the delivery of a baby.)

The corpse having been delivered to the men, in a dramatization of birth, soon afterwards conception is dramatized, when the chief mourner enters the round hole (representing the womb), receives the corpse from the lineage men, and places it in the niche—to be born in the other world. The earth here represents the woman, who identifies herself with it by sitting down on the bare earth while the grave is being covered up.

In other words, while the Christian funeral rites symbolize man's return to dust, Zulu rites indicate that man entered into this world through a woman and that though her he will return to the other world. This is also a reference to the emergence of the first Zulu man when the reed on the river bank became bulky and ultimately split and he came out.

She is thus in a marginal position between this world and the other world. As a child enters the mother's body at conception the woman begins to move into a marginal state. Although the child is identified with the mother, as it is dependent on her for its development both before and after birth (gestation and lactation), it is nevertheless different from her as it belongs to a different patrilineage. The mother is only a channel through which the child comes into this world. Conceptually the chief mourner occupies the same position.

One can draw parallels between birth and death by looking at the various phases of pollution (*umnyama*) (Table 2) which are recognized by different degrees of intensity.

---

[1] There were different opinions about the seniority of the twins. While some believed it was the second one, others said it was the first one. However, the relevance of the reference to the twins above is the illustration of the metaphor of the womb and the hut.

TABLE 2

Phases of pollution

Phase 1	Birth	From conception to parturition
	Death	From periodical treatment with black medicines to death
Phase 2	Birth	From birth to the disposal of the afterbirth emissions
	Death	From death to the disposal of the corpse
Phase 3	Birth	Lactation period
	Death	Mourning period
Phase 4	Birth	Mother and child fully separated after weaning
	Death	Chief mourner and deceased fully separated after mourning period
Phase 5	Birth	Child a full member of this world after first sacrifice
	Death	Deceased a full member of ancestral world after integration sacrifice

This can be illustrated as a curve of rising intensity during the different phases of pollution in both situations of birth and death. From conception to childbirth the pollution is believed to gradually increase, and this is demonstrated by much greater withdrawal from the public arena by the pregnant mother. The intensity is on a high plateau from parturition until the mother stops bleeding; it fades away during lactation as the baby gradually feeds more and more on solids and less on the mother's milk.

If a death is preceded by a long-drawn-out sickness, the patient is periodically treated with black medicines. During the treatment all the members of the family are also treated, and while being treated they observe *ukuzila* behaviour whereby people withdraw from society. This means that death is often preceded by phases of pollution during treatment with black medicines. The curve would start with treatment with black medicines, reach its high intensity at death to burial, and fade away until the end of mourning (Fig. 4).

In order to get a clearer insight into the meaning of pollution I shall examine other instances in which a woman is placed in a special and perhaps dangerous category.

One is the institution of divination. This is likewise an instance of a woman's marginality, as she is a point of contact between "this world" and "the other world". The diviner is not polluted with "darkness" (*umnyama*). On the contrary she is in a state of light and purity. Her problem is how to reconcile her state of purity (*unamakhosi*, being with ancestor spirits) with the profane world she lives in. Her whole behaviour is governed by this awareness.

She also goes through three phases, but in her case not phases of impurity but of purity. The first phase begins with the manifestation of her contact with the spirits—when she dreams of them, hears voices whispering in her ears, prefers solitude, neglects her appearance, eats very little and chooses the food she eats, has an urge to go and plunge

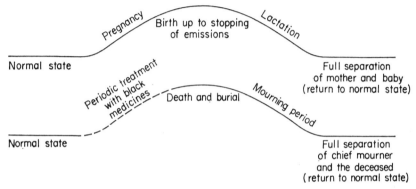

Fig. 4. A curve reflecting the degree of intensity of pollution.

herself into the river (where she often sees a huge snake that coils around her, which other people, however, do not see), and finally runs away to a diviner to be trained as an *ithwasa* (neophyte).

Being a neophyte marks her second phase, during which she withdraws from society almost completely. She devotes most of her time to ecstatic experience by singing spiritual songs of her own composition to which she dances. The whole effort is concentrated on promoting her closer contact with the spirits. A series of sacrifices and treatment with white medicines all aim at promoting her illumination. For the same reason she is painted with white clay and has ablutions twice a day. The intensity of contact is measured by the extent of her clairvoyance. She is notionally in a process of becoming permanently pure and full of spiritual power. When her training is completed she has attained the maximum clairvoyance which means that her contact with the spirits has reached its highest point. This marks her third and final phase.

She maintains her state of purity by various observances such as constant sacrifices and avoidance of all situations that are regarded as unclean. She maintains her ascetic and ecstatic experience by singing and dancing and moving more in the circles of the diviners. She is in general considered a moral and upright person, and she endeavours to live up to those expectations. It is very rare, for instance, to find a diviner being accused of sorcery, while on the other hand male doctors, who practise medicine but are not diviners, are readily accused.

While a mother experiences pollution phases of fluctuating intensity, a diviner's acquisition of spiritual contact increases in intensity until it reaches a maximum where it remains on a constant plateau.

The diviner remains permanently marginal. This is expressed by her attire, more particularly the white strips of goat skin strapped crossways over her breasts. These are intended to protect her against the dangers of non-diviners.

The argument I gave above, about the mother and the chief mourner being channels through whose bodies spiritual beings cross from the other world to this world and from this world to the other world, applies also to the diviner, who is a point of contact with the spirits who return to this world. Through a woman the transition of spiritual beings is made. This point is crucial in that it explains why diviners are women and why men must become transvestites to be diviners.

The diviner, however, belongs to the same patrilineage as the spirits that possess her, whereas a mother or a mourner is an affinal relation of the spiritual beings with whom she is in contact.

If we use Durkheimian language and regard "this world" as profane and the "other world" as sacred, the sacred world for the Zulu could further be qualified as "sacred with spiritual power over the living", and "sacred with no spiritual control over the living." The "sacred and powerful" would in this sense refer to the desired ultimate, which is the ancestral spiritual body, while "the sacred and powerless" refers to the incomplete spiritual states represented by the unborn and the recently deceased.

A woman as a "mother of birth" (umdlezane) and a "mother of death" (umfelokazi) is not dangerous only because she is marginal. She is also dangerous because she is impure. Her impurity arises from the fact that she straddles this world and the section of the other world which is sacred but powerless. The diviner on the other hand is pure, and her purity arises from the fact that she straddles this world and the section of the other world which is pure and powerful. Figure 5 illustrates this concept.

I find the basic contrasts in the Radcliffe-Brownian sense between normal and abnormal useful in gaining a better understanding of the marginality of a woman as a diviner on one hand and as a "mother" of birth and death on the other.

"Abnormal" conditions are signified either by having too much or too little, by being too strong or too weak, or by being excessively clean or excessively dirty.

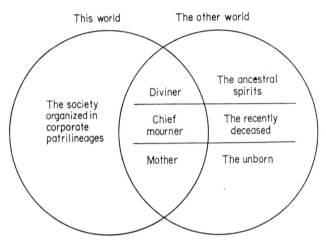

Fig. 5. The marginality of the women who represent the overlapping of "this world" and "the other world".

In this sense the diviner's purity, representing excess of spiritual power, confronts the mother's impurity, which is a deficiency of spiritual power. There is a paradoxical conjunction of these two apparently opposite extremes, in that as each of them is an index of abnormality they cannot live properly with normal people who strike the balance between the two extremes.

The contrasts between diviner and mother are shown in Table 3. This Table may give the impression that the diviner and the mother are two different people. This may be true for an unmarried girl who may be a diviner, but she ends up by being a mother. In most cases that I know of, women were possessed, or at least became neophytes, when they were already married. This means that a woman who is a diviner has the responsibility of coping with a double role—of diviner as well as of mother.

TABLE 3
Contrasts between the diviner and the mother*

Diviner	"Mother" of birth and death
Excess of spiritual power	Deficiency of spiritual power
Daughter and sister	Wife and mother
Not polluted	Polluted
Protects herself from pollution by society	Protects herself from further pollution by society
—	Protects society from her pollution
Permanent purity	Temporary impurity

*These categories inevitably reflect the male concept of women vis-à-vis men.

I shall return again later to the diviner, the mother, and the mourner. At the moment I want to examine the role of a woman not as a link between "this world" and "the other world", but as **a** link between one patrilineage and another, and see to what extent her role as wife compares with her role as diviner, mother, or mourner.

The most vivid analysis of the social situation that arises from marrying women of other lineages in patrilineal societies is given by Fortes (1970). He makes a distinction between the external aspect of lineage structure and its internal aspect which I find useful and relevant to my thesis in connection with women.

He points out that a lineage is a corporate group seen from outside, and in external relations between lineages the spouses represent their natal lineages as corporate units.

Although a lineage is a corporate group from outside, it however has a segmented internal structure which arises from the exogamous system of marriage.

To explain this Fortes uses the term "filiation", which in its primary sense means "the fact of being the child of a specified person". In this sense filiation in contrast to descent is bilateral. But this does not imply equality of social weighting for the two sides of kin connection. Correctly stated, Fortes continues, the rule should read that filiation (on the non-descent side) is always complementary unless the husband or the wife is given no parental status or is legally severed from his or her kin.

In analysing this further, Fortes writes:

> Complementary filiation appears to be the principal mechanism by which segmentation in the lineage is brought about. . . . What is a single lineage in

relation to a male founder is divided into segments of a lower order by reference
to their respective female founders on the model of the division of a polygynous
family into separate matricentral "houses". . . . Since the bilateral family is the
focal element in the web of kinship, complementary filiation provides the essential
link between a sibling group and the kin of the parent who does not determine
descent. So, a sibling group is not merely within a lineage, but is further distinguished by reference to its kin ties outside the corporate unit. This structural device allows of degrees of individuation depending on the extent to which
filiation on the non-corporate side is elaborated.

pp. 87–88

A woman in a patrilineal society such as the Zulu provides a bridge
which links through kinship ties some members of one corporate unit to
another corporate lineage unit. In other words, in a polygynous family
the man's children are united as siblings, but divided by their maternal
relationship. This means that while a woman on the one hand represents her own lineage and forms a bridge between it and the lineage
of her affines, on the other hand within the latter she forms boundaries
and not bridges—boundaries between her own children and those of her
co-wives, or between her children and those of her husband's brothers.
In this sense she is a threat to the continued unity of the corporate
group.

Her marginal position is manifested by the fact that jurally and legally
she is under the control of her husband's group, whose ancestors also
partially protect her as a wife; but her own lineage ancestors continue
to protect her as a daughter. If she becomes a diviner she is possessed
by her own ancestors even if she is married.

The result of this situation is that while members of the descent group
into which she is married are enjoined by religious sanctions against
practising sorcery to harm one another, such sanctions do not apply to
her, because, not being a full member of her husband's group, she is
out of reach of the complete and entire control of his ancestors. With
regard to sorcery, only secular sanctions apply to her. Since one cannot
be charged with sorcery unless there is adequate evidence, it is logically
safe to practise sorcery so long as one is not found out. But one cannot
hide an evil deed from the ancestral spirits.

This means that within the extended family only married women can
practise sorcery without fearing the consequences of ancestral punishment. Notionally every married woman within the homestead is a
potential sorcerer, and particularly a threat not only to her co-wives
but also to their children.

In this sense women do not only represent points of segmentation and therefore a threat to the integration of a corporate group. They also threaten the continuity of the lineage in that sorcery between co-wives or brothers' wives is often said to aim at depriving the victim of children.

In the social context, open accusation of sorcery is an index of social relations that are about to be severed. It can therefore be argued that a woman as representing the points of segmentation reflects a sorcery image, since she threatens the well-being of the corporate descent group.

This suggests that while the social structure places a woman as a wife in an ambiguous position, religious notions further isolate her as a source of danger.

The question therefore arises: Why is the society making such demands on women? The answer can be found in the type of "power" involved in each given situation.

Leach, in his paper on the "Nature of War", says this in relation to power:

> Society, however we conceive it is a network of persons held together by links of power. . . . Viewed in this way power does not lie in persons or things, but in the interactions between persons and things that is to say in *relations*. . . . Power, the influence of relationship, is ambivalent. On one side it is dominance; on the other submission. In human affairs one man's advantage is always balanced by some other man's disadvantage. Power in itself is amoral, bringing benefits to one, disaster to another. But from the point of view of the individual, power always lies on the outside; power is the influence I have on others, the influence others have on me. It is what joins me to the others, it is betwixt and between, and it is dangerous stuff. . . . On a grander scale, the same is true of society; we recognize what we are as a community, by seeing how we differ from, and how we are related to, the others.
>
> 1965, pp. 168–169

This logic of discrimination does not only lead Zulu to make category distinctions such as "our lineage" versus "other lineages", or "this world" versus the "other world". There is also a special category of persons, namely diviners, wives, mothers, who have the very important function of forming a bridge between this world and the other world, as well as between our lineage and their lineage. Their role in this respect is shown in Table 4.

In relation to the first category, i.e. our lineage linked by our wives to their lineages, the ideology is that men exercise jural and legal power over the women. This means that men are dominant and women submissive. But the power of men is challenged by the fact that women who are from outside their lineage do divide them. This is a manifestation of power which contradicts the ideology of submission and marginality associated with womanhood. It is this contradiction that is dangerous and is cast in terms of sorcery operating within the homestead.

In relation to the second category, namely "our" wives as a link between "our" lineage in this world and "our" lineage in the other world, I shall consider the other form of power that men have in contrast to women.

TABLE 4

The role of women as "bridges"*

1. "Our" lineage	"Our" wives who are marginal because they are daughters of other lineages.	"Other" lineages
2. "Our" lineage	"Our" wives (or mothers) as channels through whom our children enter from the other world and through whom we return to the other world.	"Our" lineage in the spirit world
3. "Our" lineage in the spirit world	"Our" daughters who are diviners through whom the other lineages benefit	"Other" lineages in this world

*These categories inevitably reflect the male concept of women vis-à-vis men.

A very important fact indicating the potency of man is that he has control of the reproductive fluids. While a woman menstruates involuntarily, a man usually ejaculates the semen when he voluntarily has sexual intercourse. In this sense he is in complete control of the situation. This suggests that semen is equated with potency. Therefore, if a man plans to undertake an uncertain risky enterprise tomorrow, he will not have sexual intercourse with a woman tonight, as he needs all the power he can acquire. Hence it is not surprising that men are said to abstain from sexual intercourse before such undertakings as going out to war, performing a sacrifice, going out hunting, and forging spears (in the case of a blacksmith). All these occupations are the prerogatives of males and the indices of their power. It therefore makes sense that men should abstain from activities which entail loss of semen—loss of power (i.e. energy, virility, strength).

That the woman's place is submission while that of a man is dominance is demonstrated by the ceremonial wailing (*isililo*) already mentioned (p. 84). Weeping and wailing are associated with helplessness and therefore submission, while power is demonstrated by courage and aggression. Whereas women wail, men mark the end of mourning for themselves by performing an aggressive act, namely the ritual hunting (*ihlambo*).

The hunting rites parallel the head-hunting raids of the Nagas of Assam and Dyaks of Central Borneo analysed by Leach:

> Whenever a distinguished individual dies, the whole local community must go into mourning and submit to various kinds of ritual restraints. The young men must go out on a head hunt before those mourning restraints can be removed. The head hunt itself is simply an organised raid on some neighbouring group, the objective of which is not to conquer but to kill. Evidence of the killing is provided by bringing back the skulls of the dead. . . . The close link between the physical aggression and sexual aggression is plainly manifested in various details of the associated rituals. The head hunt is felt to be an expression of male virility, a fertilizing, health-restoring act of a magical kind.
>
> 1965, p. 167

So is the Zulu ritual hunt, which is said "to clean the spears"—spears that are symbols of aggression, which stab in attack to destroy life, in a sense comparable to the phallus which stabs to create life. The rite of washing the spears lifts the ban on sexual intercourse which was in operation since the occurrence of death. In other words, what is "cleaned" and made safe to use is not only the spear but also the phallus. It is the assertion of male virility and male power.

This brings us to the position of a homicide. From one point of view he is a "hero", because he has demonstrated his power by aggression. But from another point of view he is sick; he is dangerous, polluted and marginal, not only because he has vented his power on another person as in an act of sexual intercourse which makes him weak and vulnerable, but also because by taking a human life he has identified himself with women through whom human life leaves this world for the other.

A further insight into pollution may be obtained by looking at Zulu ideas of patriliny. I quote here the explanation that was often given to me.

Inkosikazi yamukela ithathe uhlamvu olukhula lube
The woman receives, takes in, the seed which grows to be
yingane—njengohlamvu   lommbila   okuthi ngemfudemalo
a baby—just like the seed of the maize which because of the warmth
venhlabathi   evundile,   luqhume lumile.
of the soil which is fertile, germinates and takes root.

Ingane   eyendoda   ngoba iyona   etshalile.
The child belongs to the man because it is he who has sown.
Inkosikazi umhlabathi, njengoba ufaka ummbila   phansi
The woman is the soil, as you plant the maize in the soil
bese umila.   Uma umhlabathi ungavundile ummbila
it germinates. If the soil is not fertile the maize seed
awumili.
does not take root.

This suggests that as long as a man is potent he is not considered sterile. If there is no issue it is the woman who is said to be infertile. This explains the elaborate rites and sacrifices associated with marriage, most of which are intended to make the bride fertile. It is the duty of her father to perform such rites towards his ancestors to ask them to make his daughter fertile.

Here we again meet with a paradox where a man who is powerful and manifests it by his virility is dependent on the fertility of a woman. This means that a woman who is ideally submissive and powerless nevertheless exercises some power in that the continuity of the descent group depends on her fertility. I believe it is the realization of this fact that makes a woman's emissions, which are a manifestation of her reproductive powers, particularly dangerous to men's virility. They are a reminder of men's inadequacy in entirely controlling the situation of reproductivity. Women in this sense are ambiguous because they exercise some power that they should not have, and as such they are dangerous to those who are entitled to that power.[1]

I return now to the significance of reproductive emissions. Compared with the other bodily emissions, they are a class apart. As long as one lives, one defecates, urinates, produces saliva, tears and mucus as part of the body's functions. But the flow of menstrual blood and seminal fluids can dry up and stop, and still a person continues to live. The cessation of such emissions, however, would arrest the continuity of the society. Concern over the reproductive emissions is concern not only over the good health of the living, but over the replacement of the generations.

If the society is to be perpetuated it must have the means of maintaining life, i.e. food. Hence pollution affects not only the people but also their main means of livelihood, which is cattle and crops.

[1] See also Gluckman (1972, pp. 11–25).

That the reproductive emissions are a class apart becomes much more meaningful if they are contrasted with the "power" associated with the other types of emissions. Urine and saliva have a positive power of cancelling out evil. Mucus, sweat and faeces are dirty in the physical sense, but they are not polluting. I must, however, mention here that, as "body dirt", all bodily emissions can be used negatively by a sorcerer to harm. In this sense all emissions have a form of power if used for harmful purposes.

In regard to emissions I must also mention that death itself means emission of the essence of life, or the spirit from the body. A descent group as a corporate unit can be said to experience in the metaphysical sense the emission of the essence of life whenever one of their number dies and they become polluted in their capacity as a unit, while women of the lineage concerned become polluted in their capacity as mothers.

It may seem unusual that mother's milk, which is white and also food, is considered as representing pollution, when in many societies it represents goodness. A nursing mother is associated with the baby in a special way, and the baby's life is very dependent on her. If the mother's milk is regarded as a manifestation of the dependence of the descent group on the affinal relation, then its ambiguity is understandable.

This links up with the fact that the white colour, which represents what is good, can be used to represent excessive goodness or excessive power which is abnormal. For instance, a neophyte has ablutions twice a day and is covered with white clay. A diviner has white strips of goat skin permanently strapped over her shoulders and breast, all meant to promote purity. In this sense the white clay and the mother's milk both represent abnormal marginal situations. One stands for excess of power, while the other represents deficiency of power.

There is yet another point that requires some consideration. This concerns the expectation that birth and death will follow the natural patterns. We have already seen how catastrophic deaths intensify the degree of pollution brought about by death. It is this line of thinking which makes involuntary nocturnal emissions require special cleansing ritual, because semen is expected to be emitted in sexual intercourse. Further examples which are not necessarily polluting, but which fall within the same category of thought, are provided by the birth of twins or a child that is born partially covered by a membrane. The twins are identified with the spirits and referred to in the form reserved for addressingth em (*amakhosi* ancestors). They have incense burnt to them as if they were spirits. They are said to be much more sensitive to infection and prone to illness. In this sense they are in the same position as the diviner—as they have excess of power, but must live within the polluting and profane world. A child born with a strip of membrane round its body is said to be specially chosen by the spirits to be a diviner. The strip is referred to as *umnqwambo*, the same term used for the skin strips worn over the chest by the diviner.

What is meant by all this is that if birth or death does not follow the natural pattern it is regarded as abnormal and has either excessive power or deficiency of power. Zulu share this type of thinking with many other societies. Shakespeare represents it well in Macbeth when the witches told Macbeth that "no man born of woman" would have power to kill him. And, indeed, he was killed only by Macduff, who was "not born of woman" as he was a caesarian baby. What is meant here is that since Macduff was not born in the natural way he was abnormal and had excessive power over those who were born naturally.

I must also mention here that Zulu distinguish between categories of avoidances. A menstruating woman will avoid cattle and the cattle byre and will not eat milk food. So will a newly married woman. But the latter does not abstain because she is polluted, but because she is an affine, who may not have anything to do with the cattle or milk of her in-laws until the appropriate rites have been performed. If she commits a breach of avoidance she may be disciplined by being sent back to her own home to be given further instructions with regard to proper behaviour, or the ancestors may punish her. In other words legal or religious sanctions operate in the case of a newly married woman, while in the case of a menstruating woman some other mystical force which is outside the control of the ancestors operates, and her breach of proper conduct does not only affect her but may also affect the whole community in that the udders of milking cows dry up and the cattle cease to multiply. A person is not polluted because she has "sinned", but she "sins" and is automatically punishable if she does not observe a proper behaviour pattern when she is polluted.

It is important to stress that the punishment meted out by "mystical force" of this nature is experienced by the transgressor alone and not by any other person. The punishment, as I have already mentioned, is manifested in a form of neurosis which makes the transgressor a social misfit.

One is punished for deliberately exposing other people, stock and crops, to one's pollution irrespective of whether they belong to the same descent group as oneself. "Sinning" in this context cuts across the descent group boundaries.

This is in sharp contrast with punishment administered by the ancestors on their descendants, in that here the sinner is not often personally affected, but someone close to him is, as, for instance, when a child or wife falls ill as a result of transgressions of a father or a husband, or when all the inmates of a homestead experience various misfortunes because one of them has angered the ancestors. In addition, the ancestral wrath operates only in cases of violation of proper behaviour towards the members of the descent group. The ancestors are not interested in what their descendants do to people outside the group. Even in matters relating to the group the ancestors can be open to manipulation, as exemplified by lineage sorcery, when a man can persuade them to favour him and abandon his brother.

By contrast the "mystical force" is not open to any manipulation. The breach of proper behaviour by the polluted is not only automatically punishable, but once administered it cannot be reversed. The "mystical force" is concerned with the well-being of the whole society, and it operates in situations closely connected with procreation. Its sanctions therefore guarantee the continuity of the society and the replacement of generations.

Although in explaining the operation of a "mystical force" of this kind Zulu often said "the punishment happens automatically of its own volition" (*kusimde kuzenzekele*), I am nevertheless inclined to believe that such a "force" could derive from the Supreme Being.[1] If we accept this observation, then we must modify the general assertion that in societies where the veneration of ancestors is strong the Supreme Being is remote and removed from the day-to-day lives of the people. The degree of remoteness cannot be very high among the Zulu if we consider how all the time there are some people, mainly women, who, in their manifestation of procreative and reproductive capability, are engaged in an interaction with a special mystical force, since pollution is understood to be more particularly associated with situations which mark the beginning and the end of life.

These situations are associated with married women, who fulfil the important social role of forming a bridge between the two worlds, and

---

[1] I did not research extensively or intensively into the nature of such a mystical force and its relationship with the Supreme Being. More research is still required in this field.

as such they are in a condition dangerous not only to themselves as individuals but also to other people.

They are dangerous because they are marginal and ambiguous; their existence generates doubt about the difference between normal and abnormal, health and sickness; they represent as it were "gateways to death", which is indeed evidenced by the fact that in the sample of 161 cases of infant mortality, 57 (36 per cent) are attributed to the mother's vulnerability during gestation (see Appendix in Chapter 7).

So, new ritual boundaries have to be set out "to close the gate", to establish a new boundary between the truly normal world and the uncertain world represented by an individual in a marginal state.

Hence the use of insulating materials, e.g. the newly delivered mother and the chief mourner are covered up in a blanket. Later on the newly delivered mother (*umdlezane*) paints red ochre on the exposed parts of her body—the parts that have contact with the ordinary world. She does this in order to protect herself from the dangers to which she is prone and also because she herself is liable to be a channel of danger to others. By observing the right behaviour she sees herself as engaged in a procreative activity to benefit the society as a whole, while at the same time by such behaviour her freedom of movement in terms of space and time is controlled, this putting an extra stress on her subordinate role as a woman in a male dominated society.

6 | Treatment of Disease

In this chapter I shall deal with the presentation of illness, people who prepare medicines, the preparation of medicines, the various methods of administering medicines, and the classification of medicines.

Presentation of illness

Usually when a person experiences a pain he reports it to those around him. They may then observe symptoms, associate them with a definite disease, and decide whether it is a minor ailment which would readily respond to home remedies or a serious illness which requires expert handling.

In most cases the behaviour in illness is determined by the severity of the attack. A sick person may feel the pain but go on with his tasks. Such a person is said to be sick "but he goes about with it" (*uhamba nako*). But if a person has to lie down (*ulele phansi*) this suggests something serious, and those around him become alarmed and concerned. Malingering is treated with great contempt and no self-respecting person would do it. As soon as a person can get up, he is expected to do so, for it is believed that lying down, unless absolutely necessary, weakens the body, whereas getting up and moving about helps towards recovery. A patient is expected to take pain unflinchingly. For instance, a woman in labour who bears down without uttering a sound is congratulated and complimented, but one who cries out disgraces herself and her close relatives.

If what has been considered a minor ailment persists or worsens in spite of the home remedies, an outside opinion is sought, either by taking the patient to a Western-trained doctor, or consulting a Zulu practitioner (*inyanga* or *isangoma*) or a faith healer. There is no definite pattern followed at this stage, as the behaviour depends on the serious-ness of the disease, the availability of particular health agencies, the financial position, and the person who makes decisions.

Important decisions, such as consulting a Zulu doctor or diviner or taking the patient to the hospital, are made by the homestead head. In his absence those subordinate to him may get medicines to relieve pain or even consult a Western doctor; but they cannot take major decisions without his knowledge. I stress this point of his role in sickness, because in a migrant labour situation such as prevails among the Nyuswa most homestead heads are not at home most of the time. This may be one contributory factor in cases of delay in taking action to treat the patient.

A sick person is given attention day and night. It is the people of his immediate family who nurse him. The doctor may give orders that debar outsiders from coming anywhere near the patient. This is par-ticularly the case if the latter is given treatment with "black" or "red" medicines (see below, p. 110). Outsiders who visit a patient thus with-drawn speak with members of the family only in the other house or a room not occupied by him. If some family members are in a state of pol-lution (*umnyama*), such as may arise from menstruation, confinement or contact with death, they may not come into the house where a with-drawn patient is lying ill.

A sick person is encouraged to eat, as eating is believed to strengthen the body and promote a speedy recovery. Soft foods such as pumpkins, and liquids such as fermented corn meal, are preferred for a very ill person who has no appetite. If a sick infant refuses to eat, such liquid food is forced down its throat in a special manner known as *Ukaxaka* (i.e. holding the infant's nose so that it breathes through the mouth, which is held open while the food is poured in).

The practitioners

While the preparation of some herbal medicines is common knowledge, there are special medicines that are prepared only by the Zulu medical practitioners[1], male (*inyanga*) or female (*isangoma*).

[1] I shall use the expression "medical practitioners" to refer to both *inyanga* and *isangoma*, and the term "doctor" to refer to *inyanga* alone, as contrasted with "diviner" for *isangoma*. I shall use the term "Western doctor" for Western-trained doctors.

A man who wants to be an *inyanga* ("doctor") gets himself apprenticed to a practising *inyanga* for a period of not less than a year. At the
end of his training he pays his master a cow or its equivalent in money,
usually not less than R20. Sometimes a doctor passes on his skill to one
of his sons who shows an interest in medicine.

Diviners, who are usually women, share a comprehensive knowledge
of medicine with the doctor (*inyanga*). A person does not choose to
become a diviner (*isangoma*), but is said to be chosen by her ancestors,
who bestow upon her clairvoyant powers. A neophyte learns about
medicine from a qualified diviner to whom she is apprenticed for some
time, but in addition some medicines are said to be revealed to her by
her ancestors.

I have already mentioned that the ancestral spirits do not take
possession of the body, but they are close to the diviner—they "sit"
on her shoulders and whisper into her ears.

In the Nyuswa area there are three main divination techniques
according to which diviners are classified.

There is the "head" diviner or ecstatic diviner (*isangoma sekhanda*), so
called because she divines by "listening" to her ancestors, and uses no
material objects. Her clients are expected to cooperate with her by
indicating agreement or disagreement. This may be done by clapping
hands loudly when she says what they accept as the truth, and softly if
she is far from it. Some diviners prefer verbal agreement instead, such
as "I agree, I agree, I agree" (*Ngiyavuma, ngiyavuma, ngiyavuma*). This is
said enthusiastically when the diviner is driving towards the truth, and
less so when she is not.

A "head" diviner may also throw bones. In that case she is known
as "the bone thrower" (*isangoma esichitha amathambo*). From the shape
and position of such bones she can tell the unknown. While a "head"
diviner puts herself in an excited mood by sniffing certain powdery
medicines that induce sneezing and yawning, a bone thrower does not
create a special atmosphere before divination.

Bone throwing is not a prerogative of the diviners alone. It can be
learnt as an art, and as such can be practised by male doctors who are
not possessed by the ancestors. The difference, however, between the
two is that while the male doctor learns the art, it is said to be revealed
to the diviner by her ancestors. In Nyuswa, bone-throwing is more often
practised by the diviners than by the doctors. Unlike the "head"
diviners, a bone thrower is not given clues by assent or dissent while she

divines. A person may be able to practise both bone throwing and "head" divining. In that case the clients choose the technique they want to have used.

The third technique, regarded as the highest in the graded scale of divination, is that of the "whistling great ancestors" (*abalozi, amakhosi amakhulu*). The ancestral spirits in this case communicate directly with the clients by whistling out words which are meaningful to the listener. The whistling sound (ventriloquism?) comes directly from the rafters of the thatched roof, particularly at the upper part of the rondavel hut opposite the doorway. The diviner in the meantime sits almost in the centre of the hut facing toward its upper part, i.e. with her back to the doorway. If the clients are unable to understand some of the whistled words she interprets them. The clients are free to ask questions of the whistling spirits (*abalozi*), and the spirits reply. The clients never provide clues. A diviner possessed by such ancestors is said to have great ancestors (*amakhosi amakhulu*).

In cases of private consultation or which involve minor issues, a "head" diviner or bone thrower either locally domiciled or living outside the area may be consulted. But in cases of open conflicts, such as that mentioned in Chapter 3, a diviner who has whistling spirits, and who is not locally domiciled, is consulted. A bone thrower of great repute, who must likewise be an outsider, may also be consulted as, like the whistling spirits, she is not given clues.

This suggests that in consulting a diviner a number of factors are taken into consideration. In cases of private matters or minor issues the client seeks an assurance from the diviner. He already has an opinion, but he wants it confirmed. What is divulged at the session, particularly if it involves other people's names, is treated with great confidence. It is therefore not important whether the diviner is a local one who may know the situation already or if she requires clues to guide her to the desired conclusion. But for a serious issue that may lead to social rifts and public condemnation, a diviner from outside the area is ideal, because she does not have to live with whomsoever she accuses and therefore she does not make enemies with her neighbours. In addition, her clients are confident that she will not be biased as she has no relations with the litigants and no previous knowledge of their social situation.

The fees charged by diviners are graded in accordance with the technique used in divination. The "head" diviner usually charges 25c or a small chicken. The bone thrower charges slightly more, usually 50c or a larger chicken. The diviner who has the whistling spirits is the most expensive, her charges ranging from R10 to R20.

The lower charge of the ecstatic diviner (or "head") diviner is obviously based on the fact that she depends very much on the co-operation of the client. The ventriloquist on the other hand expects more payment, because she is usually consulted in very controversial issues and her divination is part of the legal system and as such is a public undertaking. This places a heavy weight of responsibility on her. In addition she will have had a longer period of developing the spiritual contact that enables her spirits to relate to her in a special way at a higher level. This means additional time spent in training, as well as additional expense in terms of animal sacrifices required during the period of training. Furthermore, the ventriloquists are fewer in number and far apart. They can therefore afford to sell their expertise at their own price.

A diviner has as comprehensive a knowledge of medicine as a male doctor. But her rates as diviner and as medical practitioner do not overlap. People consult her as a diviner in the first place to find out the cause of trouble, and they may then decide to enter into a new contract with her by hiring her to correct the trouble in her capacity as a prac-titioner. They may decide instead to get the services of a male doctor (*inyanga*). The diviner herself as part of her divination may suggest that the clients consult "such and such" an *inyanga* or may advise that they consult a Western-trained doctor. She may also name the medicines to be included in the treatment by any doctor consulted or by the client's family doctor.

Male doctors and diviners in their capacity of medical practitioners have standardized charges, which depend on the nature of the cure they are expected to effect. In treating serious illnesses such as serious abdominal and chest disorders, a practitioner guarantees cure and will be paid a cow or an ox or an equivalent sum of money only on the recovery of the patient or, in cases of a barren wife, when she has con-ceived. However, a small fee of R2.25 (*ugxa*) is paid before any treat-ment is started. If the patient dies, or becomes worse and is taken to some other medical agency, thereby terminating the services of the practitioner, the latter forfeits his final fee (even if the patient later recovers).

People need not always hire the services of a practitioner. They may instead buy prepared medicines from one for a definite ailment. In that case they pay for the medicine only.

In cases where there is no illness, but need for a prophylactic treatment such as that given in spring (*ukubethela*) to fortify the home and inmates against lightning and sorcery, or after building a home on a new site, a sum of between R10 and R20 is the usual fee. The treatment is normally completed in one day, and payment is always made in cash on that day. If the people concerned are not prepared to pay, or haggle over the sum required, the treatment becomes ineffective.

A medical practitioner treats a patient at the latter's home. He may make a number of visits if the illness is long drawn out and may even stay a few days. Occasionally he may decide to remove the patient either to his own home or to a relative's if he fears that local conditions are not conducive to a speedy recovery. This is usually understood to mean either that a sorcerer has access to the patient or that the home premises are too "charged" with the sorcery buried or scattered by him. (I see this as an ingenious move to remove the patient from a possible difficult social situation. The practitioner, who is free to spend some time at the patient's home, gets an opportunity to observe as an outsider the social situation surrounding his patient and to gauge the extent of tension and anxiety that may be contributory factors to the patient's illness.)

If the patient is removed to the practitioner's home there is usually an arrangement made whereby food will be provided for him and if he is very sick a member of his family accompanies him to nurse and cook for him. Of five patients I have known thus living at a practitioner's home, only one was too seriously ill not to attend to domestic chores.

Medical practitioners never treat themselves or any member of their family in cases of serious illness. They consult someone else, according to the Zulu saying that "A doctor never doctors himself" (*inyanga ayizelaphi*). This rule also applies to the diviner who never divines for her family or close relatives.

In addition to the doctor (*inyanga*) and the diviner (*isangoma*) there are specialists whose skills concern the preparation of medicines for a particular type of illness, or a technique to handle a particular situation related to health. Such a specialist is referred to as *inyanga* of such and such a disease (e.g. *iunyanga yomhlabelo*, the *inyanga* who handles fractured bones). Specialization is not confined to any particular sex and the skills are a family prerogative. A specialist passes on his skill to only one member of his family (or lineage segment) in the following generation, so that even within the family such knowledge is limited to one or two people at a time. Some examples of specialized skills are: the preparation of snake bite antidotes, dental medicines, treatment of fractures, the preparation of ante-natal medicines and the technique of dealing with difficult labours or breech delivery.

There are also medicines which are common knowledge, used particularly for minor ailments and as household remedies. These are usually in the form of green herbs. The countryside at Nyuswa, particularly the low bushy veld referred to in Zulu as *ehlanzeni*, has a variety of herbs. The natural bush is consciously preserved. Trees may not, for instance, be cut down unless it is absolutely necessary and permission has been given by the headman. Herbs, however, are freely collected. Although such bushy areas produce a variety of wild plants, they do not provide all the medicinal herbs required by the practitioner. To meet this need, there are herbalists in the towns who sell herbs they have collected from the countryside. Herbs not available within the Nyuswa region are obtained from such town herbalists.

Herbal medicine

Herbal medicines[1] consist of green leaves, bark, roots, stems, bulbs, fruits, flowers and seeds. Some are used in their green, fresh form, others are dried and preserved and may also be ground into powder.

Herbs may be used undiluted and applied directly on the sore or the painful part of the body. Examples of this are provided by the *umthuma* fruit (bitter-apple tree),[2] which in its green form is cut in half and rubbed directly on the ring-worm patch causing an itching sensation. In cases of ear-ache the green leaves of *isikholokotho* (*Sanseviera thyrsifolia*) are warmed over the fire and the juice squeezed into the ear. For tooth-ache a leaf paste of *ubuhlungwana* (*Wadelia natalensis*) is inserted into the decaying tooth to decrease the pain. Some herbal pastes are plastered over open wounds or ulcers. In the powdered form herbs may be used for sniffing to induce sneezing and cure headaches, or they may be taken dry on the tongue as is done with snake-bite antidote (*ubuhlungu benyonka* or *izibiba*), or they may be applied dry on the sore or ulcer, as

---

[1] See also Bryant (1970). From manuscript dated 1911.
[2] Botanical names given by Doke and Vilakazi in their Zulu/English Dictionary.

in the case of a certain fever that is believed to eat away the tissue at the rectal orifice and produce a gaping aperture. This is said to be particularly common among babies. It is considered highly dangerous as the baby need not show any signs of serious illness. The condition is referred to as *isilonda somkhuhlane* or *somoya* (the sore of the *umkhuhlane* or of the air—gangrenous rectitis?). It may also be referred to as the "thief" because it is usually not observed until too late. Whenever a baby has a cold or is feverish the rectal orifice is watched, and if it shows signs of inflammation, powdered medicine known as *umphumputho* is blown dry through a reed into the rectum to rest on the raw inner layer and effect healing. Powdered medicines are also rubbed on scarifications made on painful parts, as in the case of sprains.

Many herbs are crushed and boiled, and the decoction is sipped (*uKuphunga*) in small doses from time to time. *Iboza* leaves (*Moschoeza riparia*) are often used in this way for coughs (*ukukhwehlela*) associated with the common cold. For other, more serious chest troubles, such as short breath arising from asthma (*isifuba somoya*) or heart disease (*uvalo*), a compounded decoction of herbal medicines is prepared. Such herbal medicines are intended to soothe, heal, and clear the mucus in the chest.

In cases of stomach disorders and abdominal pains, herbal purgatives are usually given orally. A generic name for all forms of purgatives is *imbiza*. Some purgatives are reportedly used to reduce the excess quantity of gall that is believed to cause most stomach disorders. Some are very strong and may not be taken by pregnant women, as they might induce abortion. One example is *uhlumguhlungu* (species of peppery shrub—*Vernonia corimbosa*). In cases of diarrhoea, purgatives are generally used in the belief that it is essential to clean out the cause of the diarrhoea from the system, and this is usually followed by binding medicines such as the leaves of *umvuthwamini* (*Plectronia ventosa*) which are pounded and taken with milk or porridge.

Although many purgatives are taken orally there are also many purging enemata, particularly in cases of abdominal pains. Liquid herbal medicine is injected per rectum, and the dosage is controlled so as to enable the patient to keep it inside for a time. During this time the medicine is believed to draw out undesirable substances from the internal abdominal organs. Rubber syringes are now replacing cow's horns used by adults for enema or reeds used for babies. A woman whose menstruation is accompanied by pain (*isilumo*) has *isidwa* roots (*Gladiolus ludwigii*) pulverized and boiled, and administers this as an

enema. A barren woman is also usually treated with purgative enemas
"to clean out the womb" by removing substances obstructing conception. This treatment is referred to as *ukugeqa* (like scooping out the
contents of a gourd). (Medicine may also be introduced directly into
the womb in order to clean it out.)

In addition a wide variety of herbs are used for enemas. The most
popular for mild stomach disorders at Nyuswa is *ikhambi lesiduli* (*Cardio-
spermum heluacabum*).

An emetic is another common technique of cure, particularly in cases
of illness that affect the chest. In cases of *idliso* sorcery (harmful substances in the food), the harmful substance eaten is believed to embed
itself or settle in the chest region. To correct the condition such a substance must be taken out by an emetic.   Very often emetics are used
just as expectorants to relieve the chest by clearing air passages. They
are also used widely as a corrective in cases of feelings of nausea, general
debility, or body pain believed to result from excessive accumulation
of gall, which comes out as a bitter greenish or yellowish substance.

Ideally an emetic is taken warm on an empty stomach in the early
morning. Some emetic medicines make a person sick and come up on
their own, others require inducement by irritating the throat with a
feather or finger. Warm water is provided for drinking, more and more
between vomits, to clear the stomach of all emetic medicine. Only older
children and adults are treated with emetics as it is a strain for younger
children. The technique has to be acquired by practice; thus children
under the age of, say, 12 are not thought capable of carrying out the
treatment.

In cases of feverishness, a steam bath (*ukugquma*) to induce perspira-
tion and reduce fever is provided for adults. The patient is made to
kneel naked over a pot containing a boiling hot mixture of herbs. He
is covered with a blanket. After such steaming he is kept warm and
given more herbal medicines to sip.

A fomenting treatment (*ukuthoba*) is usually applied on painful parts,
as in cases of rheumatic muscular pain or of aching or swollen feet. A
mixture of herbs is boiled and allowed to cool a little so that it does not
scald the skin when applied on the sore part. A rag is usually dipped
into the hot medicine and pressed on. Poultices may also be applied in
the form of heated herb paste or a paste of hot corn porridge, particularly in cases of boils, to facilitate the formation of pus.

Blood letting is sometimes resorted to, to relieve pain. Blood cupping (*ukulumeka*) in cases of severe headaches is one example. *Ukuchachaza* (to let the blood drip) is another. It is done in cases of pregnant women who have oedema. In the seventh or eighth month the women is taken to the river where she lies flat on her back on the river bank. A specialist, who has tied *insekane* grass around her index finger, rolls the finger round in the woman's vagina. Since the grass has sharp edges it cuts the skin, which bleeds. If the haemorrhage does not stop, the woman is dipped into cold water in the river. The shock of the cold water is said to stop the bleeding. This treatment is intended to reduce the danger of still-birth or premature birth.

Classification of medicines

The herbal medicines (*amakhambi*) described above are believed to contain healing properties and are administered independently of any ritual context. If found ineffective they are discarded for better ones. Such medicines are used to cure somatic symptoms.

The medicines I am going to describe now are administered in a ritual context and have a symbolic meaning. In the main they are used for prophylactic purposes or to correct the cause of illness rather than to cure the organic symptoms. Medicines of this class are also principally herbal (*amakhubalo*). *Amakhubalo* are essentially dried bark and roots. The term also means compounded medicines prepared only by professional practitioners and prescribed by them. The ingredients of such a mixture may include *izinyamazane* (wild animals), medicines derived from wild animals (as the term suggests) in the form of fat, pieces of skin and feathers. These are said to cure the effects of dangerous wild animal tracks.

Such medicinal compounds can be divided into three colour categories:

1. Black medicines (*imithi emnyama*).
2. Red medicines (*imithi ebomovu*).
3. White medicines (*imithi emhlophe*).

The medicines that are classified according to their colour are further terminologically distinguished. For instance, there are:

a. *Ubulawu*, liquid medicine used as black, red, or white emetics. Emetics that have no colour significance are never termed *ubulawu*.
b. *Insizi*, powder produced from charred herbs, roots or animal medicine. It always belongs to the black class of medicines.

c. *Intelezi*, liquid medicine that belongs to the white class of medicines. It is said to possess the special quality of rendering the evil
effects of sorcery ineffective. For instance, if sprinkled on a spot
where a sorcerer is believed to have buried or placed harmful substances it nullifies the power to harm in such substances. The *intelezi*
type of medicine differs from other white medicine in that it is never
taken internally. It is either used to wash with or to sprinkle with.
Most people plant species of this type at home in order to ward off
evils of all kinds.

Treatment with such symbolic medicines is intended to correct the
cause of illness, and is characterized by a notion of "taking out the
bad" from the system, "discarding it" outside the premises, and
re-introducing good health. To elucidate these symbolic features I shall
now describe two instances of such treatment; space does not allow me
to recount all those known to me.

To correct the effects of lineage sorcery a treatment is performed
known as *ukuguqula amanzi*—literally, "to turn round the water", i.e. to
change the effects of black watery medicine that caused the ancestors
to abandon the patients.

A black sheep is killed by suffocation (*isimuku*) and placed unopened
in a hole dug outside the homestead, preferably in secluded bushy surroundings.

Black medicine, consisting of a mixture of chopped up fresh roots,
bark, stems and leaves, is prepared by the doctor. The mixture is boiled
in water to produce darkish liquid stuff, which is placed in a clay pot.

Before dawn, the homestead head stirs the medicine with a twig
until it froths. All the adult members of the homestead drink their fill
of this and vomit over the dead sheep. This is repeated for three days.

During those days the people concerned withdraw from society and
abstain from pleasurable experiences (*ukuzila*). They are considered as
having an intensified form of pollution (*umnyama*). They are dangerous
to other people, as this form of *umnyama* (pollution) is transferable. The
others are also dangerous to them, as in their vulnerable state they could
contract diseases from those people.

To conclude the treatment with black medicines, the clay pot that
contained them is thrown with the remnants of the medicines on to the
carcase of the sheep, where it breaks into fragments. The whole thing
is well covered with stones and thorny branches.

On the morning of the fourth day after dawn when there is light, the patients use white medicines as an emetic. These are also herbs, that are chopped up, pounded, and steeped in cold water. Such a mixture of white medicines is never boiled. The homestead head stirs the medicine, which is in a clay pot, until it froths. While doing so he speaks to the ancestors, telling them of his problems and requesting them to look favourably towards him and his dependants. Every adult member smears the white froth on face or limbs, and they all use the white medicines to vomit in the cattle byre or anywhere else within the premises. On the same day a white goat is slaughtered as in the manner of a sacrifice. It is eaten during the three days of treatment with white medicine. This treatment does not involve *ukuzila* behaviour, and the people rejoin society and resume normal life again.

A similar example is provided by the use of red and white *ubulawu* medicines to remove the type of *umnyama* known as *isidina*. This is the condition of people who feel they are unpopular or even that they are looked upon as repugnant.[1] The condition may be accidentally contracted in the environment or be caused by a harmful substance said to have been deliberately placed by a sorcerer. To correct it a decoction of red *ubulawu* is prepared. After boiling, it is reddish in colour. The mixture is divided into two and kept in two different clay pots (or tin containers). One container is used for steaming purposes and the other for emetics. For steaming, the mixture is brought to a boiling point and the patient kneels over the steam covered with a blanket, until he sweats profusely. It is for this reason that the steaming medicine is kept separate as the sweat falls into the medicine and thus it cannot be used for emetics. The emetic mixture is stirred with a short twig until it froths. The patient takes as large an amount of this as he can manage, and vomiting is induced outside the homestead before dawn. After vomiting, the patient takes a mouthful of the mixture, and squirts it out, saying *hamba bubi* (go away evil!), *hamba sinyama* (go away blackness!). The steaming and vomiting are repeated for three consecutive days. On the third and last day what remains of the medicine is thrown away at crossroads and frequented pathways (*endleleni yomendo*, highway). During treatment with red medicines, abstinence is observed, but much less strictly than when black medicines are used. After this, treatment begins with white *ubulawiu* for three consecutive days. Cold water is added to a mixture of herbs, which is allowed to stand for a while before being

[1] Young men who find themselves unpopular with girls usually resort to this treatment.

used for emetics and bathing only and not also for steaming purposes. Early in the morning the medicine is stirred until it froths. While stirring it, the patient addresses the ancestors, stating his wishes and his problems. (This is significant in that it gives an opportunity for a minor to address the ancestors in his own right.) He rubs the white froth on his face and arms. Vomiting takes place at home in daylight. Later in the day the patient adds the medicine to his bath water. This is repeated for three days. The remainder of the medicine is scattered within the premises and in the cattle byre.

The above examples indicate that various things are expressed by the treatment. In fact it is no exaggeration to say that there is an embarrassing wealth of symbolic expression. I cannot delve into all this here, it could be the subject of a book in its own right. However, since the more prominent symbols are expressed in colour representation, I shall in the following chapter focus my attention on colour symbolism.

7 | Colour Symbolism in Medicine

The two instances of mystical treatment described in the last chapter indicate that colour plays an important and dominant role in symbolism related to treatment of mystical illness. The important symbolic colours are black (*mnyama*), red (*bomvu*) and white (*mhlophe*). They are used serially in that order. The sequence is rigid and is never reversed. Black and red are said to be equivocal, in that they stand for both goodness and badness; white represents only what is good. Because black and red share certain attributes one of them may be omitted, in which case we either have black followed by white or red followed by white. The important fact to note is that whenever black or red is used it must be followed by white, whereas white can be used alone without being preceded by either of the others.

Treatment with such coloured medicines is initially intended to establish a balance between a person and the environment. Once such a balance is established, it must be sustained by another treatment if it is thought to be waning, and if it is lost it must be regained.

Both black and red are used to expel from the body system what is bad and also to strengthen the body against future attacks. Ridding the body of what is bad and undesirable does not mean that a person is in good health. To regain good health white medicines are used.

In the following analysis I hope to show how and why each of the three colours is believed to possess "power" of a different kind.

Many anthropologists have already observed that relations which exist in nature are apprehended by the human brain and used to generate cultural products which incorporate the same relations. In like manner I believe the Zulu colour symbolism is related on the one hand to the cosmic order of day and night, and on the other to the bodily functions of eating and defecating.

There is ample evidence in everyday expression indicating that the colour symbols are related to or associated with the cosmic order of day and night.

Night is *ubusuku*, and the darkness of the night is *umnyama*. *Umnyama* is a term also used for pollution, and polluted people are said to be without light and in the darkness (lit. *banomnyama*, they are with darkness).

A Zulu term for black is *-mnyama*. But, in fact, the correct English translation of *-mnyama* is dark/black, as there is no Zulu terminology to discriminate between the two.

White is associated with light, but unlike *mnyama* (dark/black) the terminology discriminates between the two. White is *-mhlophe*, e.g. *amazinyo amhlophe*, the white teeth; light is *ukukhanya* as a noun and *-khanya* as a verb, which means "to be light", "to be bright", "to shine forth", and "to be white". White and light, however, in certain contexts are used to mean the same thing. To illustrate this I give here a text related to the nubility rites I observed.

The first sacrificial animal, a white goat, was brought into the main hut and made to stand towards the upper part of the men's side. It was held facing east and Malezi, the celebrant, stood next to it also facing east. Her father held the goat by the neck, and calling upon his ancestors said:

Nangu umntwana wenu uMalezi
Here is child yours Malezi
Ngiyamemulisa
I perform nubility ceremony for her
Akube mhlophe konke
Let it be white all
Izindlela zakhe zibe mhlophe
Pathways hers be white
Kukhanye,   abone
Let there be light, let her [be enabled to] see
Kudeduke   umnyama
Out of her way be darkness

Abe   nezinhlanhla
Let her be of good fortune
Azale   abantu
Let her bear people
Ahlale   kahle
Let her live well
Aphile   kahle
Let her health be good
Kube   mhlophe konke empilweni yakhe
Let it be white all in life hers

In this passage light and white are used to mean the same thing. In explaining "Pathways hers be white" (*izindlela zakhe zibe mhlophe*), the celebrant's mother said it means that her future life must be bright. "Pathways" is used here to indicate that one progresses forward in life as one walks forward along pathways.

The emphasis is that "there must be light and no darkness". The good things of life, good health and good fortune, are here associated with light, which is also represented by white.

It is during the day that people participate in social activities, that they live their lives. They depend on the light of the day to see. In the darkness of the night they cannot see, and if one cannot see all sorts of dangers may lurk. During the night, people withdraw from social activities. Sick people become sicker, and sorcerers are said to be at work performing their anti-social practices. Ancestral spirits are believed to visit their descendants in their sleep and through dreams make their wishes known. Sleep is *ubuthongo*, and an ancestral spirit is *ithongo*. The etymology here could well indicate the contact during sleep between the living and the dead, in which case sleep may be regarded as a miniature death that takes a person away from the conscious life of the day. While the darkness of night is dangerous, it is nevertheless necessary to enable people to withdraw and rest in order to be fresh for their life activities on the morrow. Herein lies the relevance of the equivocal power of black medicines. While they are dangerous, they are nevertheless necessary to make a person strong and powerful.

Day and night are, however, divided by the twilight of sunrise and sunset. The twilight is a reddish dim illumination, which at sunset becomes progressively dimmer and at sunrise becomes progressively brighter. Red is *-bomvu* (e.g. *igazi libomvu*, the blood is red).

Unlike "black" and "white", "red" (*bomvu*) is not used in everyday expression in its moral sense to describe misfortunes and blessings. This is understandable, for life situations are thought of as either good or bad. The dim twilight represents the "between" position, where the dimness represents something of darkness as well as something of light. Because light is pure and unambiguous, red is identified with black, even though black and red do not represent the same things. Red compared with black represents less danger and more good. This is demonstrated in many ways. For instance, in cases where only black and white treatment is performed, something of the white medicines is added at some point to the black medicines. This is said to minimize the period of neutrality—of being neither sick nor healthy—which is associated with the in-between stage in treatment when black medicines are stopped to be later replaced by white medicines. It is, however, unnecessary to add white medicine to the last red medicines, because red medicines have goodness in themselves which bridges the gap between red and white treatment. This is further indicated by the fact that during treatment with red medicines the stringent abstinence that accompanies black medical treatment is relaxed, which suggests that less danger is associated with them.

Although red is not as explicit as black and white in expressing misfortunes and good fortune, it is nevertheless an important member of the colour-symbolic triad, as there can be neither day nor night without the reddish twilight.

The daylight represents life and good health. To be (mystically) ill is likened to moving away from the daylight into the dimness of the sunset and on into the night. The sorcerer is believed to use black medicines that represent the darkness of the night. The practitioner endeavours to drive a patient out of the mystical darkness by black medicines, through the reddish twilight of the sunrise by red medicines, and back into the daylight and life by white medicines. This cycle is shown in Fig. 6.

To regain the lost mystical health involves a process of movement from one point (night) to the other (day). The method of cure with black, red and white medicines should be accordingly looked upon as a continuous process (or transformation), rather than as an opposition between black and white. If viewed in this way it explains the rigid sequence of colour symbols.

There is one other colour that shares certain semantic characteristics

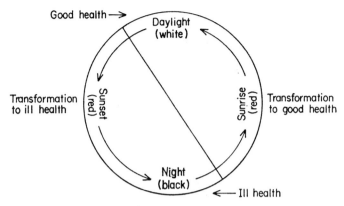

Fig. 6. The relationship of colour symbolism with cosmic order of day and night.

with these three. This is -*luhlaza*, "green/blue". The vegetation, the sea, the water, the sky are -*luhlaza*. The term is also used to mean raw, unripe and uncooked. This is obviously associated with the fact that fruits are green (-*luhlaza*) in colour when unripe.

Black, red, white and green/blue are the only colour terms that can be used with ideophonic extensions to establish the exactness of colour.

Black = *mnyama*

> *Kumnyama khace* It is very dark (as of the darkness of night)
> *Kumnyama bhuqe* It is pitch black (as of coal)
> *Kumnyama tsu* It is pitch black (as of coal)
> (The ideophones in each case denote that it cannot be blacker or darker.)

White = *mhlophe*

> *Kumhlophe qwa* It is immaculately white (as of cloth)
> *Kumhlophe nke* It is sparkling white (as of teeth)
> *Kumhlophe wu* It is completely white (as of white hair)
> (In all cases it is emphasized that the whiteness is complete; it cannot be whiter.)

Light = *khanya*

> *Kukhanya bha* It is brilliantly light (as of daylight)
> *Kukhanya nge* It is brilliantly light (as of daylight)
> (This means it cannot be lighter.)

Red = -*bomvu*

Kubomvu klebhu It is bright red (as of blood)

Kubomvu tsebhu It is bright red (as of blood)

(The ideophones indicate the brightest red.)

Green/blue = *luhlaza*

Kuluhlaza cwe[1] It is clear green/blue (as of the sky or of fresh green leaves)

Kuluhlaza tshoko It is bright green/blue (as of fresh green leaves)

(The last ideophone is often more used with reference to vegetation and not so much with sky and water, as it also may be used for "raw".)

The ideophone *cwe* which describes green/blue (*luhlaza*) emphasizes the clearness and purity of the colour, and in this form green/blue *luhlaza* is identified with white in the symbolic language. Water is green/blue (*amanzi aluhlaza*), and water is always used in the white contextual sense. Some treatments may not be performed if the sky is overcast, because the (green/blue) sky is regarded as an important white symbol.

I emphasize here the importance of purity and clearness of green/blue (*luhlaza*) because the darker shades of green/blue can be classified as black. This is also the case with all other colours, which symbolically may be classified in accordance with whether they are darkish, reddish or light. Green/blue in its clear and pure form is classified with white not because it is lightish, but because of its pure and clear form, recognized even in bright green which is by no means lightish.

That there is one colour term for green/blue does not mean that there is no recognition of visual differences between green and blue. If there is need to specify, such differences are expressed descriptively, e.g.

It is as green/blue (as the sky) (*Kuluhlaza njengesibhakabhaka*).

It is as green/blue (as grass) (*Kuluhlaza njengotshani*).

It may well be that green and blue are expressed in one colour term because of association with what the daylight reveals. The green landscape, the green/blue Indian ocean and the blue sky are the most

---

[1] Doke and Vilakazi, Zulu/English Dictionary translations. *Cwe* (ideophone): Of blueness, greenness, clearness. *Kuluhlaza cwe* (It is bright blue): *Amanzi athe cwe* (The water is clear). There is also a verb *cweba* derived from *cwe*, which Doke and Vilakazi translate as: Become clear, pure, fresh, quiet, peaceful, green, blue. It is significant that the Catholic Church in South Africa has adopted *cweba* to mean holy or saint, e.g. Holy water: *Amanzi acwebileyo*; Saint Mary: *uMaria ocwebileyo*.

prominent visual objects, which merge on the horizon to form a unit coloured -*luhlaza*. It may also be possible that green/blue is identified with white because of this association with light. Daylight reveals the natural surroundings, which are mainly green/blue.

White (*mhlophe*) and green/blue (*luhlaza*) are the only two colours that have no association with substantives. Black (-*mnyama*) is associated with darkness (*umnyama*), and red (*bomvu*) is associated with red ochre (*ibomvu*).

The rest of the colour terms are also the names of objects that have the colour, and they cannot be used with ideophonic extensions like those already mentioned. These are:

Brown, *nsundu*, associated with the *isundu* palm tree and its brown fruits (or dates), which are also known as *amasundu*.

Yellow, *phuzi*, associated with the light yellow coarse pumpkin called *iphuzi*.

Grey, *ngwevu* or *mpunga*. Both words mean a mixture of black and white hair. They more specifically mean a grey-headed person.

Pink, *mpofu*, also tan and tawny colour, associated with the colour of the eland skin. The eland is *impofu*.

Orange, *mthubi*, the thick yellow milk of a cow after calving is *umthubi*.

Purple, *nsomi*, the reddish winged starling bird is *insomi*.

It may be useful at this point to look once again into the symbolic meaning of mystical treatment such as that intended to correct lineage sorcery (see above, p. 110).

The suffocated sheep represents natural human death, where a person dies without being wounded. It is buried like a corpse. Both the medicine and the sheep are black, and the treatment is performed in private during darkness of night to symbolize darkness and death. During the course of treatment people withdraw from society and avoid all pleasurable experiences to symbolize the withdrawal of the dead from the social life of the living. The extraction of what is bad from the body by black emetics, and discarding it secretly away from home, is related to excretion, which is expelled as dirt from the body and discarded in the wilderness outside the home. The sheep in this context may be looked upon as a "scapegoat" which receives all that is discarded as evil.

The white goat that accompanies white medicines is an antithesis of the black sheep. It represents life, as people come together and share in the meal. It represents daylight and social activity—and it brings together in a special way both the living and the dead. White medicines, like the white goat, emphasize light and life. Because they are meant to bring good health into the system, as well as all the good things of life, one vomits at home to bring the good things within reach. It is done in the morning at daylight. Eating together the meat of the sacrificial goat, and performing white treatment in the open, in daylight, represents eating itself, which is life-giving and good, an antithesis of excretion represented by black treatment.

Whereas the black symbols represent excretion, death and darkness—all of which is anti-social, the antithesis of society—the white symbols represent life, eating and light, which all epitomize society and provide the canopy of social action.

The goodness contained in the black medicines is symbolized by the white froth that comes up when it is beaten. The white froth is not used, however, but it is brought out as an indication of the equivocal nature of blackness. By contrast, with white medicine the froth is smeared on the face and arms to emphasize the goodness of the medicines. That the treatment represents a transformation that is a process—progressing from the darkness of night to the goodness of daylight—is indicated by the fact that after treatment with black medicines in the wilderness people do not look back. They leave behind what is bad and proceed to the future that is good.

There is in addition another set of symbolic meanings that operates within the colour symbolism. This is related to the notions of heat and cold. Illness is associated with heat. Black (and red) medicines, which represent illness, are always heated: they may be boiled, burned into cinders to form black powdery medicines, administered as smoke arising from burning them, or heated in a container into which people dip and then suck their fingers. In the two instances described in the last chapter (see pp. 110–112) the black emetic is a decoction, while the white medicine is an infusion.

The above symbolic language demonstrates how a cluster of symbols can be superimposed and operate simultaneously. For instance, the symbols as related to cosmic order and as related to the body function of eating and excreting are expressed simultaneously by the same performance as expresses the concept of heat and cold. In other words three things happened at the same time: (a) there is restoration of the balance—which is the removal from the darkness into the light;

(b) there is the "thing" taken out of the body by black (or red) medicines, and the "thing" taken in by white medicines—the taking in, and the taking out represent defecation and eating; (c) there is the cooling of heat, heat being represented by black or red medicines while the cooling is represented by white. In this last category there seems to be more emphasis on what is uncooked than on what is cooked. I was often told (and indeed also saw) that the black and red medicines are "cooked" (*iyaphekwa*) and the white medicines are "not cooked" (*ayiphekwa*), that is they are taken raw (*iluhlaza*). There is the double meaning here of the word *luhlaza*, which on the one hand means green/blue and stands for "goodness" and on the other means what is raw or uncooked. This aspect conforms to the Levi-Straussian division of Culture and Nature. The cooked black and red medicine represents the cultural element, which also embodies the moral element of losing one's mystical "balance", either by failing to maintain and sustain it or by falling victim to sorcery. In other words being mystically sick is culturally acquired. To correct the condition black and red medicines are cooked, and to re-establish the natural state of life treatment with uncooked medicines is given (Levi-Strauss, 1970; Leach, 1970).

In addition, colour as a dominant symbol provides a model that makes it possible to identify the meaning of a symbol by the way it is used, even if it is not necessarily coloured black, red or white. This is well demonstrated by the sacrificial symbols.

The blood that comes out of the fatal wound is regarded as of special importance. Such blood is referred to as the wound (*inxeba*)—the wound that makes possible the important contact between the living and the dead, the wound that takes animal life to give life to the sacrificing group. It is a bridge that links the living and the dead (the profane and the sacred). In this sense it is consistent with the red symbolic meaning in medicine, where red is a bridge over which the sick are brought back to life. The spear or the knife used to kill the animal is carefully guarded so that it does not fall into the hands of an enemy who might scrape off the blood and use it in sorcery to nullify the sacrifice. The blood on the spear or knife is especially important compared with the rest of the blood in that it represents the very first sign of bleeding. Although it is on the weapon and not on the wound it is nevertheless metaphorically referred to as *inxeba*, the wound.

The other important sacrificial portions are associated with the digestive tract. They are the bile (*inyongo*), the chyme (*umswani*) and the third stomach (*inanzi* or *incekwa*).

The gall bladder is removed and closely guarded until it is used. In the nubility sacrifice mentioned above (p. 114), on the day following the sacrifice Malezi, the celebrant, stood in the main hut while the bile was sprinkled on the floor to encircle her. She then stepped out of the circle, facing the east. The rest of the bile was sprinkled on the big toe of her right foot and the index finger of her right hand. She also swallowed a bit of it. The empty gall bladder was inflated and she wore it pinned on her head during the rest of the ceremony. Afterwards she kept it, as she would wear it again on her wedding day.

I was told that the spirits like the taste of gall—they lick it. If sprinkled on the celebrant she is sure to be in contact with the spirits in a special way. Sprinkling it on her finger and toe was said to make her future life white and bright. The future here is symbolized by the index finger, which permanently points forward. All the bad and dangerous things that might threaten her life she leaves behind incapsulated within the circle as she steps out into the bright light of the future (*ukukhanya nezinhlanhla*, the light and the good fortune). I was emphatically told that the gall has "white" attributes and therefore stands for all that is good, usually represented by white.

Hyman says, writing on "Comparative Vertebrate Anatomy":

> The caecum (i.e. the third stomach or *inanzi* in Zulu) lies at the junction of small and large intestines. Mammals usually have a conspicuous caecum which may in herbivorous forms be very long and large in which case it assists in digestion and absorption.
>
> 1922, p. 263

Nyembezi and Nxumalo (1966, p. 51), writing in Zulu, describe *inanzi* (caecum) as a tube about one foot long in which there is fluid dung that oozes out when removed from *inanzi*. (*Ingumbhobho omude ocishe ube yifide, phakathi kukhoma ubulongwe obumanzi okuthi lapho umuntu abukhipha buphume buthi tshu.*)

This last description suggests the observation of the metamorphosis of grass in the animal's stomach. Zulu may have a limited knowledge of general anatomy, but they have names for every internal part of a goat or a cow. It is not surprising therefore that the sacrificial symbols suggest a good knowledge of digestive stages.

In order to appreciate the significance of the digestive tract in ritual, let us remind ourselves that in order to live we eat. When food enters the body it is considered clean, but it is excreted as dirt.

In a goat or cow, the third stomach (caecum) represents a point where the digestion and absorption is less active. It is the last stage before what has been food becomes utterly rejected as waste matter. The important point to note here is that what is in the third stomach can be regarded as food even though it has overtones of dirt.

In sacrifice the third stomach is hung at the upper part of the main hut. It is left hanging while the rest of the meat is consumed. When at last it is cooked, it is eaten by the oldest woman of the family or lineage segment, a woman who has reached her menopause.

The third stomach is said to be saturated with the ancestral presence as it has a longer contact with the spirits. I was told that it is eaten by old women only because the saturation with spiritual presence would interfere with the reproductive powers of younger women. This explanation makes sense only in the light of the meaning of black, red and white symbolism. I have already mentioned that the gall sprinkled on a nubile girl is believed to associate her very closely with the spirits and this is regarded as good, and yet if she ate the third stomach it would do her harm. I believe the explanation for this lies in the fact that the gall and the third stomach represent two different forms of "power". The gall stands for whiteness, which is unequivocally good, while the third stomach represents what is almost dirt, and therefore black and dangerous.

If the animal is killed for ordinary feasting, the intestines and the stomachs, including the caecum, are reserved for married women of all ages.

I must also mention here that the meat of the sacrificial goat, always killed a day before the ox sacrifice, is eaten only by the members of a lineage segment. It can be viewed as a sacramental meal in which all the descendants participate. But the caecum is considered special, an extraordinary sacramental meal.

William James, in his book on "The Varieties of Religious Experience" (1952, p. 161) points out that most complete philosophies must find some ultimate way of affirming that which has been rejected. He further continues:

> It may indeed be that no religious reconciliation with the absolute totality of things is possible. Some evils, indeed, are ministerial to higher forms of good but it may be that there are forms of evil so extreme as to enter into no good system whatsoever, and that, in respect of such evil, dumb submission or neglect

to notice is the only practical resource. . . . But . . . since the evil facts are as
genuine parts of nature as the good ones, the philosophic presumption should
be that they have some rational significance, and that systematic healthy-
mindedness, failing as it does to accord to sorrow, pain and death any positive
and active attention whatever, is formally less complete than systems that try
at least to include these elements in their scope. *The completest religions would
therefore seem to be those in which the pessimistic elements are best developed* [my italics].
Quoted from Mary Douglas, 1966, p. 165

The third stomach (and indeed black symbolism) represents "that
pessimistic element which is best developed", while the large intestine
which contains what is regarded as too dirty represents "that form of
evil so extreme as to enter into no good system whatsoever". In Mary
Douglas's garden metaphor, the third stomach is "like the weeds which
a gardener turns into compost to make the garden good".

With regard to the first stomach, Hyman (1922, p. 263) says: "The
stomach (or ventriculum) follows the esophagus as a spindle shaped to
sacci-form enlargement provided with enzyme and acid secreting
glands . . ."

The chyme in the first stomach represents a point of contact when
the vegetable matter is acted upon by the animal matter in order to
make absorption, which is a life-giving process, possible. The special
ability of the body to make use of the food is a "power" that is real and
almost demonstrable.

The power represented by the chyme is different from that of the
third stomach. The chyme is still intact with all the life-giving food
properties, although it also contains what is potentially dirty. In this
sense it can be likened to the red symbol which although dangerous is
more inclined towards goodness.

During sacrifice the chyme is, however, an important silent member of
the digestive tract triad. It is hidden from the public and buried secretly in
the cattle byre, well mixed with cattle manure in order to be indistinguish-
able and therefore not available to ill-wishers. Meanwhile the gall is used
to isolate and identify the celebrant, and the third stomach is used as a
special communion in which the oldest woman represents the whole group.

Although the chyme is not positively or effectively used in sacrifice,
it is very demonstrably used when animals are killed for cleansing purposes, whereas the gall and third stomach are of no significance. I
believe this is because the chyme as representing the "life-giving
essence" is capitalized upon to get back the "life" that is threatened by
the state of pollution (*umnyama*). Whereas in sacrifice the primary

purpose is to contact the spirits, in cleansing killing the primary purpose is to rid the people of pollution. It is not surprising therefore that the gall and the third stomach, the two important animal organs through which special contact with the spirits is made, are of no significance in cleansing rituals.

Although these sacrificial symbols are related to the digestive tract, they have, at the same time, relevance to the cosmic order. In other words the cosmic order of day and night and the functioning of the digestive tract are inextricably linked concepts. For instance, the gall as food for the ancestors is green/blue (*luhlaza*) like the grass that is food for the sacrificial animal—food which sustained its life—life which is symbolized by green/blue, white and light. The bile therefore represents life, while chyme is used to represent what red symbols stand for, i.e. transformation, and the third stomach represents what black symbols stand for, i.e. negative attributes of life.

Understanding the meaning of these sacrificial symbols not only throws light on how a model of colour symbolism can help to reveal the significance of symbols outside the colour spectrum. It also enables us to realize that where symbols are not strictly medicinal in usage, they need not be sequential, but can be juxtaposed and expressed simultaneously, or there can be an orchestration in which different people express different symbols that are part of a unit. This cannot be better represented than in sacrificial symbols, where the old woman represents the negative attributes of life by eating the caecum, the celebrant is sprinkled with gall to indicate the desired state of life, and the two, along with all the other members of the descent group, partake of the communal sacrificial meal. Such orchestration is common in non-medicinal symbols. (During the first fruit ceremonies the King was painted with white, red and black powder to form prominent stripes—all of which simultaneously represents death, birth and life. Bryant, 1949, p. 510.)

There are certain features of the use of colour symbols among the Zulu which I want to stress more particularly in relation to the rich material on colour symbolism among the Ndembu analysed by Professor Victor Turner.

In explaining the tendency to abridge the usage of colour symbols into pairs either of black and white or of red and white, Turner suggests that black is often left out because it is negative and dangerous while "white and red on the contrary are associated with activity—both are considered 'to have power'" (Turner, 1967, p. 79).

While I agree with him with regard to the danger associated with black symbols, I find it difficult to accept that they are conceived as having "no power", since the very negative attribute they represent suggests that they have a negative influence which in itself is "power".

What I would like to add is that both black and white are capable of representing extreme situations, i.e. excessive impurity/excessive purity. In Chapter 5 we noted how a neophyte promotes her state of purity by frequent use of white symbols and thus becomes abnormally pure, in which case her situation conflicts with the normal life. To control these possible excessive situations among the Zulu there are alternative symbols, viz. red and green/blue, whereby in the case of the former some attributes of "black" are expressed and in that of the latter "white" attributes are expressed; in both cases these colours are regarded as not reaching the frontiers of extremities.

What I find significant in adding further weight to this observation is that in virtually all cases of pollution arising from life crisis situations (i.e. parturition, bereavement, gestation, lactation, homicide) Zulu use only red and white symbols. In such situations the biological experience itself is said to weaken the patient and "enshroud" her with darkness (*ambozwe umnyama*). There is therefore no further need to simulate death by black symbols, but there is need to transform the dangerous situation to "life" by using symbols of transformation, i.e. red symbols, and symbols of life, i.e. white symbols.

That red emerges as a symbol of transformation and transition is expressed in the case of treatment to correct lineage sorcery mentioned in the last chapter.

I was told that the black medicines remove the evil, the misfortunes, the darkness, all of which enshrouds the patients, and cast these on to the black sheep. The patients during this period represent their symbolic death by withdrawal from society. What I want to emphasize here is that such symbolic "death" is regarded as a "state of being dead", which is the opposite of a "state of being alive". After completion of the period of treatment with black medicines, the evil of death and danger is believed to have been removed. This notionally means that for a day between the completion of a course of treatment with black medicines and the resumption of a course of treatment with white medicines, the patients could be symbolically regarded as "neither dead nor alive". The practitioners emphasized that they have to watch out for this anomaly and bridge the gap which it creates; hence some white medicines are added to the last dose of black medication to introduce a good dose of positiveness within the predominantly negativeness of black medicines. If, however, only red and white medicines are used, as in the case of correcting repulsiveness (*isidina*) already mentioned (p. 111), no white medicines are added to the last dose of red medicines, because red medicines in themselves contain sufficient goodness to bridge the gap between red and white. Besides, red carries less danger which could create a wide gap between what these two colours represent. What this highlights is that Zulu see red symbols as representing transformation, transition, and birth, while black and white symbols represent static conditions of life and death.

I believe this is a significant subtle detail which throws some further light on our understanding of the marginal phase in the rites of passage as taught us by Van Gennep.

Turner, writing on the interstructural character of the liminal, says:

> . . . Undoing, dissolution, decomposition, are accompanied by processes of growth, transformation and the reformation of the old elements in new patterns. . . . Antithetical processes of death and growth may be represented by the same tokens, e.g. huts, tunnels, which are at once tombs and wombs. . . . The coincidence of opposite processes and notions in a single representation characterizes the peculiar unity of the liminal, that which is neither this nor that, and yet both.
>
> 1967, p. 99

The Zulu material demonstrates that it is possible to distinguish between the phases that respectively stand for "undoing, dissolution or decomposition" and "death" (black symbols), "growth", "regeneration" and "rebirth" (red symbols), and the desired things in life, i.e. good health, good fortune, place in society (white symbols).

Because among the Zulu colour symbols are prominently used in healing situations, the sequence of colour is insisted upon. It may not be quite as explicit whether among the Ndembu the red symbols also stand for transformation, since there the colour symbols are more connected with initiation and hunting rituals than with situations of illness. None the less I am inclined to believe that the Ndembu also seem to regard red symbols as symbols of transformation. Professor Turner tells us of the ambivalent nature of red symbols: in certain rituals they may be identified with white symbols, and in others with black (p. 74). I believe it is this unique quality of red symbols that makes it possible for them to represent the end of death, a negative state, and the beginning of life, a positive state. It is precisely this ambivalence that enables red symbols to represent transformation from one state to the other.

I have laboured the importance of red symbols because I believe it is a point where "true passage" in the rites of passage is expressed. I find it necessary to emphasize this because it notionally represents transformation from ill-health to good health. After all, this is what medicine and cure is all about. It is an attempt to effect a change, to move away from an undesired situation to a desired and ideal state.

I cannot leave the subject of colour without referring to the contribution made by Berlin and Kay (1969) to our understanding of the significance of colour terms. Writing on the evolution of basic colour terms, they recognize seven successive stages.

The basic term is psychologically salient for informants, indices for salience being the tendency to occur at the beginning of the list of colour terms, stability of reference across informants and across occasions of use, and occurrence in the idealets of all informants. Its application must not be restricted to a narrow class of objects and its significance should not be included in that of any other colour term. Colour terms that are also the name of an object characteristically having that colour are suspect.

In accordance with their definition of basic colour terms, Berlin and Kay conclude that all societies have terms for black and white. This is stage 1 in evolution. Stage 2 has three terms, the third being red (in addition to black and white). Stage 3(a) has green as the fourth term (extending into blues). Stage 3(b) has yellow instead of green as a fourth term. Stage 4 has five terms, including both green and yellow. Stage 5 has blue as a sixth term. Stage 6 has brown as a seventh term. Stage 7 has purple, pink, orange or grey, and this may give a total of eleven terms.

Berlin and Kay point out:

> All languages of highly industrialized European and Asian people are stage 7 while all representatives of early stages (1, 2 and 3) are spoken by people with small populations and limited technology located in isolated areas. There is also some evidence to suggest that for groups living "close to nature" basic colour terms are of relatively little adaptive value because of their broadness of reference. For example, to a group whose members have frequent occasions to contrast fine shades of leaf colour and who possess no dyed fabrics, colour-coded electrical wires and so forth, it may not be worthwhile to rote learn labels for gross perceptual discriminations such as green/blue despite the psychophysical salience of such contrasts.   p. 16

Since -*mnyama* means both dark and black, and is related to *umnyama* which means darkness, and since red -*bomvu* is related to red ochre (*ibomvu*), both red and black may not be said to be monolexemic, and they would also be suspect because they are "colour terms that are also the name of an object characteristically having that colour". Yet in the Zulu language black and red, along with white and green/blue, stand out prominently; I have already indicated the special linguistic characteristics that these colour terms share. I suggest that among the Zulu all the evidence points to the fact that these colour terms are of special importance because of their ritual significance. It therefore becomes less important whether they are primary or derived, or whether they are monolexemic or not.

I must, however, point out that black, white, red and green/blue, as principal colours seem to confirm Berlin and Kay's observation that such colours tend to be within the first three stages of colour terms.

But I must also mention that this does not by any means imply that there are no terms to represent the seven colour stages. The terms listed on page 119 express colour as understood by the speakers of the language as standard colour terms, and they are listed as such in the dictionaries (Doke and Vilakazi Zulu/English dictionary). They are related to substantives in the same sense as black and red are related to darkness (*umnyama*) and red ochre (*ibomvu*). If therefore they are not acceptable as basic colour terms because of their ties with objects of the same colour, black and red would have to be removed from stages 1 and 2, in which case the Zulu would be an exception in Berlin and Kay's finding that all societies have basic colour terms for black and white.

Berlin and Kay further explain the incidence of one colour term for green/blue in many societies as due to closeness to nature where people "have frequent occasions to contrast fine shades of leaf colour". I would expect people who so discriminate between fine shades of leaf colour to develop an even more sensitive perceptual discrimination between green and blue.

In concluding this chapter I must return to the implications of symbolic treatment. Since evil is believed to be taken out of the system as a material substance by black and red medicine, the problem that arises is how to discard or dispose of such evil substances without endangering the lives of other members of the community.

The best way of disposal, since such evil does not dissipate itself if just discarded, is to cast it on some animal in a "scapegoat" fashion.

There are various instances among the Zulu where evil is cast upon animals. For example, in cases of bereavement a goat is killed and only its chyme is used ritually to cleanse the bereaved; the rest of the carcase is thrown away (or today eaten by people who are not related to the bereaved). Another instance is that of the girls' age-sets where, if one girl is deflowered, the others are cleansed by the man responsible for the pregnancy; he offers a live goat to the girls, who set upon it, remove its chyme, and leave it to die along the riverside, where they smear themselves with the chyme and later wash it off in the flowing water. The meat of this goat may be eaten only by very old women who have reached menopause, as it is said to be full of the evil cast upon it. It is said that in the old days even old women did not touch it. The most important scapegoat of all was the black bull that featured prominently in first fruit ceremonies during the period of the Zulu Kingdom. Strips of meat from such a bull were only used medicinally to strengthen the nation with black medicine. The rest of the carcase was burnt to cinders. It was upon this bull that all the evil influences accumulated on the land during the preceding year were cast in order to start a new year free from evil. In this sense the King cleansed the whole nation and the whole Kingdom.

However, in spite of all these various opportunities of discarding evil, the problem still remains of discarding the lesser evil, the evil that presents itself between situations which demand greater efforts of substitution.

In an attempt to solve the problem, the areas most often used for disposal are cross-roads (*enhlanganweni yezindlela*) and highways (*endleleni yomendo*). It is hoped that since they are often frequented by travellers, outsiders or strangers the evil will attach itself to such passers-by and be carried away by them from the territory, thus diminishing the dangers in the immediate environment. But the problem is not quite solved. Although a stranger may carry away the undesirable element, he may also introduce dangers that he brings with him from a foreign territory. However, any such addition to the existing dangers in the countryside is counterbalanced and kept in check by the "throwing away" done at highways and cross-roads.

Although this may appear as a collusion against outsiders, it nevertheless stresses boundaries and highlights the priorities in social obligations. A man strengthens himself and his dependants, but he also considers the welfare of his fellow man in the community. The attempt to keep the locality clean spotlights the collective responsibility of the community to preserve itself first. It also spotlights faith in humanity, in that the principle of discarding what is dangerous implies that those who handle what is discarded are handling "dynamite" which they can very well use against anyone they choose to harm. Yet, despite the conflicts that arise and the enemies that a man makes, the people who are believed to practise sorcery are proportionately very few if one considers the readily available sorcery substances.

This brings to mind the responsibility of the polluted towards the community. Manifestations of certain life experiences make people recognize their state of pollution. The onus rests on polluted persons to protect those around them from their pollution.

What has emerged in this analysis is that in the causation of disease and treatment, three elements stand out prominently. There is an element of *morality*, an element of *natural* processes, and an element of *mystical* processes.

To begin with the last one, people are sometimes considered sick not because of any organic disorder, but because they undergo certain life crises and are regarded as stricken with pollution. Pollution is a mystical concept that cannot be demonstrated according to the laws of cause and effect. The correction of the condition involves mystical means expressed in symbolic medicines.

By contrast there is illness that always presents itself in somatic symptoms and is recognized as a natural process inherent in all living things whereby they break down from time to time. Illnesses of this class collectively known as *umkhuhlane*, are natural illnesses. Their occurrence is beyond the control of the patient, and he is therefore not held responsible. The medicines used for them are believed to contain properties able to cure the symptoms, and may be discarded for better ones.

Finally, there is a dimension of morality in causation of disease which is associated with social situations. For instance, the illness that arises from sorcery is an index of the sorcerer's immoral anti-social behaviour. On the other hand, however, sorcery can be thwarted by anti-sorcery measures which make it bounce off and become ineffective. When people are properly "balanced" (or in good order, *balungusiwe*) sorcery bounces off. This implies duty and responsibility towards oneself as well as towards dependants, the taking of necessary precautions to maintain a proper balance which would counterbalance sorcery as well as incidental environmental dangers. Morality also implies maintenance of good relations with the ancestors, who would otherwise withdraw their protection.

Illnesses arising from lack of balance related to a morality principle may show themselves either by misfortunes only, with no somatic symptoms, or by misfortune as well as somatic symptoms. In the case of the former, only the mystical treatment is performed, to correct the lost balance (or to get away from the situation of darkness); but in the case of the latter there will be two levels of treatment—the mystical to treat the whole person, and the empirical to cure the somatic symptoms.

An example of the two levels of treatment is provided by cases of women whose miscarriages are diagnosed by the diviner as an outcome of lineage sorcery. During the next pregnancy after her miscarriage, the woman drinks cupfuls from time to time of an infusion of pounded herbs known as *umsekelo*. This is a natural or empirical treatment. Alternatively, instead of taking *umsekelo* medicines she may prefer to consult the Western-trained doctor about her tendency to miscarry; but the mystical treatment to correct the effects of lineage sorcery would not be changed. The symbolic treatment is fixed and standardized for each mystical illness. It is not abandoned if good results are not realized, but is repeated all over again, because such rites are rites of transformation, rites of process, of passage from a mystical state of darkness to one of mystical light. Treatment in this sense is a religious act.

Although illness that involves morality in its causality implies a state of darkness or lack of balance, there are a few exceptions. *Idliso* (to make someone eat harmful substances by adding them to food in the manner of poisoning) is one instance. Although it is an immoral act it does not place its victims in a mystical imbalance and it is not open to any prophylactic treatment. It always has somatic symptoms. It is thus given natural or empirical treatment.

The relationship between the notions of causality and the type of treatment is summarized in Table 5.

The notions of black, red and white and the rigid sequence of colours in usage is frequently mentioned by writers on Zulu medicine (e.g. Bryant, 1970, p. 20; Krige, E. J., 1950, p. 328; Callaway, 1884, p. 142). Although none of the literature gives an analysis of the significance of symbolic treatment, it nevertheless indicates that the notions are neither new nor typical of Nyuswa-Zulu only, but are part of a general Zulu pattern of thought.

The treatment of disease as discussed in this chapter and summarized

TABLE 5

MORALITY

The people and their sense of responsibility (i.e. prophylactic measures to maintain balance), intentions (i.e. sorcery to put other people out of balance), duty (i.e. to the ancestors and dependents)

MYSTICAL

Lack of balance conceptualized as *umkhondo/umego* (i.e. environmental dangers) and as lineage sorcery and ancestor wrath

NATURAL

Somatic symptoms arising from vulnerability associated with lack of balance

MYSTICAL

Misfortune arising from vulnerability associated with lack of balance. No somatic symptoms

MYSTICAL

Lack of balance owing to pollution (*umnyama*) arising from reproductive phases. No somatic symptoms

Symbolic treatment only

NATURAL

Somatic symptoms arising from *idliso* or poisoning sorcery. No mystical symptoms

NATURAL

Diseases that just happen. Somatic symptoms (*umkhuhlane*)

Empirical treatment only.

Symbolic and empirical treatment

in Table 5 becomes much more significant if looked at in relation to the mythology that explains death (see p. 47). I find certain aspects of the myth interesting. That the people are given contradictory messages symbolizes, I believe, the right of people to make decisions and to take responsibility for their actions. It stands for the notions of morality (or culture) which set the human being apart from animals. That the people, the animals (represented by the lizard and the chameleon), and the plants (represented by the berry bush) are brought together in this story symbolizes the relationship of the people to their environment—it stands for the notions of that which is Nature.[1] That the people accepted orders from a "Supreme Being" presupposes the fundamental realiza-tion that there are certain things beyond man's understanding, things that are controlled outside his sphere of action. This constitutes the notion of the mystical. What I find particularly enlightening is the fact that the lizard,[2] which is greyish-brown in colour—and therefore black in the ritual sense—is sent to deliver a death message. This conjures up the idea of black "medicines" believed to be used by the sorcerer to effect the illness or even death of his victims. The chameleon, known for its ability to change colour to suit its surroundings, is sent to deliver a life message. It stops on the way to feed on mauve berries (mauve is red in the ritual sense); this reminds one of the treatment with black, red and white "medicines"—red is in the middle (half-way)—to be followed by white. Indeed, the chameleon delivered good tidings "after it had been reddish when feeding on red berries", like white "medi-cines" which introduce good health after red "medicines".

Now that we have examined causation and treatment of disease, it is perhaps time to look at the extent to which such notions are believed to operate. Some idea of that may be obtained from the statistical information that follows.

Statistical Appendix

During the first eight months of 1971 information about causes of death and current illness was collected in a hundred *imizi* comprising 1182 people of Nyuswa. They were contiguous and within a walking distance (i.e. a radius of about $2\frac{1}{2}$ miles) from where I lived while carrying out

[1] The Zulu myth has a lot in common with the Christian myth of Adam and Eve in the Garden of Eden.
[2] The salamander lizard.

my research. The inhabitants of 50 *imizi* consider the ancestor cult as their religion; those of the others belong either to orthodox Christian Churches or to African independent Churches. Despite these religious differences, the people differ very little, if at all, in outlook regarding the cause and the treatment of disease.

The data were collected mainly to ascertain the extent of fertility among women and the rate of infant mortality. The respondents were the mothers themselves or senior women of their *umuzi*. In cases of widowhood the cause of death of the deceased spouse was recorded. This was also done for children who had died as adults.

The data obtained are set out in Tables 6–9. But the findings can by no means be considered conclusive. I am very aware of the bias in collecting data of this nature. For example, if the respondent is believed by the other people of the *umuzi* to be herself responsible for the death, she would be reluctant to say so. If she is not keen to talk on such matters, the interviewer will be reluctant to probe, as death is a painful subject and people must only speak about it if they want to. The 14 per cent of "No information" in Table 8 is due partly to this fact and partly to my oversight. Another problem is that the findings of different diviners or doctors may clash. In such cases we recorded what the respondent believed to be true.

Although, for the above reasons, the figures cannot be entirely relied upon as reflecting the true situation, I am confident that they do give a rough idea of the tendencies.

TABLE 6

Number of deceased

Status	Number	%
Adults	61	24
Children (aged 3–16)	30	12
Babies (aged under 3)	120	48
Miscarriages	27	11
Still-births	14	5
TOTAL	252	100

% calculated on a round total of 250

Out of a total of 252, it was only possible to obtain information about the causes of 191 deaths because in 61 cases the cause of death was not

TABLE 7
Number of persons currently ill

Status	Number	%
Adults	73	66
Children (aged 3–16)	23	21
Babies (aged under 3)	15	13
TOTAL	111	100

% calculated on a round total of 110

TABLE 8
Cause of death

Cause	Number	%
No information	40	14
Unknown	21	8
umkhuhlane (natural cause)	24	9
Injury or accident	10	3
Umkhondo (dangerous tracks)	25	9
Undefined *umeqo* (evil tracks stepped over)	6	2
Umeqo (evil tracks stepped over) defined as sorcery	7	2
Umeqo (evil tracks stepped over) contracted by pregnant women and affecting the unborn baby	57	21
Idliso (poisonous substances added to food)	11	4
Ancestor wrath	11	4
Lineage sorcery	25	9
Life crises causing *umnyama* (pollution)	2	1
"Just happened"	8	3
Portions of sacrificial animal used in sorcery	4	2
Sorcery of other forms	13	5
Other	11	4
TOTAL	276	100

% calculated on a round total figure of 275

established. It may seem puzzling that no less than 276 causes were given to explain the deaths of 191 people This is because in some cases two factors were believed to be responsible for death, e.g. when an accident was seen as a manifestation of misfortune owing to a condition of *umnyama* (pollution) resulting from lineage sorcery, here the accident was the immediate cause of death, but lineage sorcery caused it to happen.

The figures reflect a number of significant factors. What stands out most prominently is that environmental causes (*umkhando* and the three varieties of *umeqo*) were reported in no fewer than 95 cases (34 per cent of the total).

Of those 95 cases, 82 were of babies who died as infants or were miscarried or born dead. The total number of dead babies was 161 (see Table 6). Of this number 82 (51 per cent) had died of environmental causes, mostly by contracting illness through their mother during the gestation period. This is understandable if we consider that pregnancy is believed to diminish resistance—it disturbs the balance, so the mother becomes more vulnerable. It is significant that though pollution is implied, it is not categorically named as a secondary cause of death arising from environmental changes which affect a pregnant mother. I suggest that this is because any direct reference to pollution would implicate the mothers who would, as carriers of contamination, be named as responsible for the death of their children.

This explains why there are only two cases of pollution. These were unusual cases in that normally *umnyama* arising from biological happenings is attended to and given the correct treatment. In these two cases this did not happen. The first case was that of a homicide who, because he was not given the treatment with red and white medicines, developed a condition known as *iqungo* (a lust to kill) and became a killer. Ultimately he himself was killed. He was murdered because his condition of *iqungo* exposed him to it. The second case is that of an unmarried mother whose baby died and who was not purified nor given treatment with white "medicines". When she became ill and died, the diviner pointed out that she had been an easy target for disease as she was in a state of *umnyama*.

The "just happened" cases were mainly of twins. Their death in infancy is usually regarded as "just happening—it is one of those things with twins" (*Knyazenzekela, iwele liyenda*).

By "sorcery of other forms" is meant the type of sorcery that does not

fit into the categories analysed and is not frequent enough to deserve
elaborate analysis here, e.g. the type of "venereal disease" (*iqondo*) said
to be contracted by adultery with a married woman whose husband
had placed a charm on her to trap her lover. Sorcery such as sending
lightning to strike the victim also falls into this category.

TABLE 9

Cause of illness (living persons)

Cause	Number	%
Umkhuhlane (natural cause)	23	21
Injury or accident	8	7
Umkhondo (dangerous tracks)	2	2
Undefined *umeqo* (evil tracks stepped over)	5	4
Umeqo (evil tracks stepped over) defined as sorcery	9	8
Umeqo (evil tracks stepped over) affecting unborn baby	1	1
Idliso (poisonous substances added to food)	6	5
Ancestor wrath	14	13
Lineage sorcery	7	6
Possession	3	3
"Just happened"	8	7
Sorcery of other forms	5	4
Other	12	11
Unknown	9	8
TOTAL	111	100
Current misfortunes recognized as "illness"	27	

% calculated on a round total of 110.

The "other" category (Table 8) refers to miscellaneous causality
which is not regarded as sorcery, yet also not as *umkhuhlane*. Some
examples are suicide, abortion, murder, T.B. and cancer.

It is of interest to note that the highest number (Table 9) is of patients
believed to be suffering from *umkhuhlane*. But in some cases what has been
regarded as *umkhuhlane* causes concern, particularly if it becomes fatal
and if it is one of a number of other misfortunes experienced by the

family. This suggests that what has been regarded as *umkhuhlane* may be viewed differently if the patient dies. I had experience of two such cases while in the field. This explains why there are many more cases of sickness from *umkhuhlane* than death from that cause.

Finally, 27 misfortunes were reported to constitute "illness". This is of special interest since the information was given spontaneously in response to the question: "Is there anybody ill at the moment?" This question was expected to elicit information about illness in the biological sense.

8 | Some Notions of Evil Spirit Possession

Spirit possession among the Nguni-speaking peoples of South Africa is a subject that has received a great deal of attention in anthropological literature. Bryant (1949, 1970), Junod (1927), Sundkler (1961), Krige (1936), Hunter (1947), Kohler (1941), Loudon (1959, 1965), Hammond Tooke (1962), Laubscher (1937), Lee (1969), and Marwick (1966) have all drawn our attention to different facets of this social and religious phenomenon. Since the notion of spirit possession and divination is a complex subject which cannot be given adequate attention in one chapter, I will direct my attention to what is regarded as evil spirit possession and therefore a menace to the society and see how this is related to the present-day Zulu social life.

The meaning of spirit

I shall begin by describing briefly what Zulu say are "old" or "traditional" forms of spirit possession. To understand this, it is necessary to recapitulate the salient beliefs about the supernatural world (already discussed in Chapter 4).

It is believed that the Supreme Being or God (*Umvelinqangi*) lived up above (*ezulwini*), along with the Goddess often referred to as the "Princess of the Sky" (*inkosazana yezulu*). The spirits of the deceased live down below; hence they are often referred to as "those of below" (*abaphansi*). Both of the deities who live above are remote and rarely invoked. It is the ancestors who are more concerned with the day-to-day lives of the living.

The "World Below" is thought of as divided into three sections: that of the unborn spirits, that of the recently deceased spirits, and that of the ancestors. When a woman conceives the biological event is said to be associated with the entry of the spirit from the section of the unborn. Each baby during its first year of life has a sacrifice (*imbeleko*) performed for it. By this sacrifice it is placed under the protection of its parents' ancestors. It is not only given social status by being made the child of a definite set of parents, it is also given a ticket of passage that enables it to complete the cycle of life. If the child dies before the first sacrifice is performed, the spirit is said to return to the section of the unborn. But if the sacrifice has been performed the spirit will go through the processes enabling it to join the body of the ancestors.

The expectation or rather ideal is that a person grows up to maturity, marries, has children, and dies of old age. A deceased who has had the essential first sacrifice does not, however, as a spirit directly join the body of ancestral spirits. Soon after death the spirit is said to be "in a place of wilderness" (*endle*) "in an in between state" (*esithubeni*), and is lonely and unhappy. How long this period of isolation lasts depends on the deceased's social status. If he was married, the period is about a year; if unmarried and adult, about six months; and if a baby or a child, about three months. During this period the chief mourner observes mourning behaviour. Ideally, at the end of the period a sacrifice is performed to integrate the spirit with the rest of the ancestral spirits. This is the desired complete status of spiritual being which enables the spirit to be powerful—to bless or punish the descendants.

The passage of the spirit from the world below to this world, and from this world back to the world below, is effected through married women. When a woman conceives such a transference is made, and when death occurs the chief mourner is always a married woman, who mourns the death of her husband, her children, her mother-in-law or her daughter-in-law. In this way she is associated with death in a special way, and can be said to be mother of both birth and death. However, as a wife and mother she is an outsider in her husband's lineage group, and in this position she is associated with spiritual beings that, are powerless, viz. the unborn spirit or the recently deceased, both of which have not reached a complete spiritual state.

Traditional spirit possession

The spirits that are said to possess a diviner (*isangoma*) are not the unborn or the recently deceased, but those that have reached the desired complete state of spiritual being. The spirits in their complete state as ancestors return to this world through their daughters, not through their wives, mothers or daughters-in-law. The diviner is principally possessed by the spirits of her own descent group, not those of her husband's. Divination is a woman's thing, and if a man gets possessed he becomes a transvestite, as he is playing the role of a daughter rather than that of a son. For the special and very close contact with the spirits is reserved in this society for women only—women who are thought of as marginal, and can thus fulfil the important social role of forming a bridge between the two worlds.

In possession, the spirits are believed to "ride" on the shoulders of the possessed and to speak or whisper to her. She hears voices and in that way gets her clairvoyant powers. As a diviner she avoids unclean situations and uses white symbols to emphasize her purity and her special association with the purity of the ancestral spirits.

Indiki possession

At the turn of the century a new type of possession was experienced in Natal and Zululand. It is known as *indiki*.[1] Bryant wrote in 1911 about its outbreak among the Zulu and Junod reported the same thing among the Tsonga in Mozambique in 1913. Both reported it as a new form of spirit possession.

It is still regarded as a new form of possession that is closely associated with African industrial development.

An *indiki* is believed to be the spirit of a deceased person, a spirit that was never given the necessary sacrifice of integration with the body of other spirits. The people from countries farther north who come to work in the mines of South African often die at the place of work, and their families, not knowing of their death, perform none of the rituals necessary to place them in their proper position in the spirit world. Such spirits wander about in desperation and become a menace to the local people, taking possession of them and causing illness. *Indiki* is

---

[1] The meaning of the term is not known. It is widely used in many language groups in Southern Africa where the same type of possession happens. Occasionally the term *amandawo* is used for *amandiki*. *Amandawo* seems to be a term related to the Ndjao people who live in Rhodesia.

therefore a male spirit (usually only one) who enters a person and resides in the chest. The patient then becomes deranged and manifests this by crying in a deep bellowing voice and speaking a foreign tongue, usually identified as one of the languages spoken by people in the north.

The treatment, which is always given by a diviner who was herself once possessed by *Indiki*, involves a short period of initiation into the spirit cult, about three months or less. During this period the treatment aims to exorcise the alien spirit and replace it with one of a male ancestor to protect the patient from future attacks. For this reason the initiand uses red emetics to remove the alien spirit, and white emetics to arouse her own spirit. Such emetics are used on alternate days during the whole period of initiation. In addition to using red emetics the initiand wears red symbols, such as a red wrapper around her waist or a red scarf on her head (or a red cap in the case of a man). Because her own ancestor is being persuaded to possess her and supersede the alien spirit, she observes a behaviour pattern in many ways similar to that observed by the traditional neophyte, i.e. she withdraws from society, observes various forms of abstinence, and wears white strips of goat's skin across her chest, skin wristlets, and inflated gall bladders, all of which are derived from sacrificial goats slaughtered to induce possession by her male ancestor. In addition she sings, dances and works herself into ecstasy, like the traditional neophyte. The main difference between the *indiki* initiand and the traditional initiand is that the former attempts to arouse her spirit in order to regain her health, with no intention of becoming a fully-fledged diviner for the rest of her life. The effort to become possessed is made consciously, whereas possession of the traditional neophyte is not induced. It is the ancestors who choose to possess her even against her will. She is a chosen one, chosen by the good spirits for the benefit of the society, while the *indiki* is primarily chosen by an alien, which for her is a bad spirit and must be superseded by the good ancestral spirit for her protection. (In addition, a male *indiki* neophyte does not become a transvestite as in the case of traditional possession.)

The treatment results in a spirit cult membership that gradually lapses with the passage of time or is strengthened by additional forms of accepted possession. For instance, if she belongs to an independent sect that practises an ecstatic type of worship, such an *indiki*[1] will

---

[1] Even when the alien spirit, the *indiki*, is thrown out and replaced by an ancestral spirit, the patient is still referred to as *indiki*.

promote powers of prophecy and healing; alternatively, she may further be possessed in the traditional way by ancestral spirits and become a fully-fledged diviner who will have the special ability of treating *indiki* patients.

The notion of *indiki* has caused concern about the safety of infants in an environment that is further endangered by the alien spirits. This has given rise to a new method of treating newborn babies so as to protect them against the effects of the alien spirits. The treatment is intended to arouse the baby's male ancestor (to raise *indiki*, *ukukhuphula indiki*) to take special care of the baby until it passes through the dangerous stage of babyhood. Such treatment is performed only by diviners, not by doctors (*izinyanga*). The treatment, which is usually stopped after a year or eighteen months, is known as *igobongo*, because the red and white medicines are prepared in two separate gourds (*amagobongo*). These are used on alternate days as enemas.

Ufufunyane[1] or izizwe possession

Bryant and Junod, who both wrote on the sudden spread of *indiki* possession, make no mention of *ufufunyane*, which is another form of spirit possession. This suggests that *ufufunyane* is a much later concept. It is indeed usually associated with the late nineteen twenties and nineteen thirties. It also is said to have been introduced into South Africa by people from the north.

Whereas *indiki* is contracted in the atmosphere by mere chance, *ufufunyane* is primarily due to sorcery, although chance is not ruled out as a secondary cause. A sorcerer is said to add soil from graves and ants from the graveyard to his harmful concoction. In this way the spirits of the dead are said to be captured and controlled by the sorcery. The harmful concoction may be placed on a path used by the victim, and through contact with it she becomes sick.

A person with *ufufunyane* in its worst form usually behaves as if mentally deranged. She becomes hysterical and weeps aloud uncontrollably, throws herself on the ground, tears off her clothes, runs in a frenzy, and usually attempts to commit suicide. She reacts violently and aggressively to those who try to calm her. She is said to be possessed by a horde of spirits of different racial groups. Usually there may be thousands of Indians or Whites, some hundreds of Sotho or Zulu spirits.

[1] The dictionary translation of *Ufufunyane* by Doke and Vilakazi is: "Rapidly spreading disease which causes delirium and insanity; type of brain disease, mania, hysteria".

The treatment may be given by any of the local practitioners, i.e. either a diviner (*isangoma*) or a doctor (*iyanga*). Its aim is to force the spirits out of the patient. When such spirits have been exorcized they roam the countryside in small bands and may attach themselves to people who are not sufficiently fortified against them. This is chance possession, and the attack is less violent or may manifest itself in some form of neurosis or mental confusion.

Ufufunyane spirit possession does not lead to any cult membership. It does not give any diagnostic or healing powers.

Some practitioners, in treating *ufufunyane*, install benign spirits. These are not the patient's ancestral spirits, but are spirits controlled by the practitioner. They are referred to as the army (*amabutho*) installed to protect and defend the patient against malign spirits.

There is an ailment of infants connected with *ufufunyane*. This is a condition of malformed placenta known as *ipleti* (a Zuluized form of the English word "plate"). It is said that a normal placenta is shaped like a clenched fist, whereas a malformed placenta is flat with the circumference of a dinner plate. *Ipleti* is said to have affected babies born in and since the late thirties. Many elderly women claim that only the children they had in the late thirties had *ipleti*, while those born earlier had no malformation of the placenta.

There are two ways in which *ipleti* is brought about. Firstly, if the mother suffers from *ufufunyane*, even in its mild form, her baby will be born with *ipleti*. Secondly, since the appearance of such malformed placentae, midwives, in discarding them, bury them along the main pathways; hence it is impossible for any pregnant woman to avoid stepping over one and becoming affected.

In treating spirit possession symbolic medicines characterized by their colour—these colours being black, red and white—are used. Their significance has already been discussed. White symbols (i.e. white emetics and frequent ablution with white medicines) are used by diviners to promote their state of purity, while red emetics which are followed on the following day by white emetics are used for the *indiki* possessed. The red medicines are meant to take out the alien spirit and strengthen the patient against future attacks, while the white medicines are used to restore the lost good health. In the case of *ufufunyane* patients, or babies with malformed placenta (*ipleti*), black medicines are used to throw out the spirits or to correct the effects of the malformation. White medicines are used after them to facilitate the return to good health.

Analysis

There are several things that we learn from this brief account. They can be summarized as follows.

The notion of evil brought about by spirit possession in the case of *indiki* or *ufufunyane* is conceptualized as violation of the principle of patrilineage. A spirit that takes possession indiscriminately outside the patrilineal descent principle is thus regarded as evil. The evilness inheres not so much in the spirit itself as in confusing the categories. In other words, all spirits within their proper place have no evil connotations. They only acquire this if and when they intrude. The intrusion is dramatically emphasized and underlined by the very nature of possession, in that the alien spirit actually takes "possession" of the patient by residing within and superseding the identity of his personality, so that he becomes a husk housing a spirit which speaks in its own voice from within him.

What is illuminating is that possession by such alien spirits is associated with changing social circumstances.

Let us consider *indiki* possession, for instance. The development of the mines resulted in the recruitment of workers from alien cultures north of South Africa.[1] Such men came to work for long stretches of time without their families. The danger of intrusion into the family life of the indigenous peoples can be seen in this light as real if we consider the probability of relationships developing between the aliens and the wives, sisters and daughters of Zulu men. Unions of this nature constitute a threat to the stability of the society not only because of differences in culture, but also because miners are likely to return home when their contract expires and leave their Zulu wives and children behind. In this way an element of disorder is introduced. It is significant that in treating *indiki* possession an endeavour is made to replace the alien spirit with a male ancestor. This suggests emphasis on rejection of the alien male and replacement with a native male.

Ufufunyane possession represents yet another dimension of social relations. As industries flourished, the towns developed. This meant further intrusions of peoples from overseas, more particularly when there was a great depression in Europe after the First World War. With the

[1] Although there are no gold mines in Natal and Zululand, Zulu men meet miners in Johannesburg and Kimberly. Thus, Zulu could have adopted the notion of *indiki* from other African language groups. I am recording here what the Nyuswa people told me about *indiki*.

increasing mobility and intensified migratory labour contacts between peoples of various racial groups grew daily. A Zulu became a threat to another Zulu as they competed for jobs, housing, land and economic security. The feeling of "insecurity" grew, and both Indians and Whites combined were seen as a formidable force bent on disrupting the equilibrium of Zulu society. I suggest that the thousands of spirits of various races that are believed to possess an *ufufunyane* sufferer and show their presence by violent aggression, hysteria or threat of suicide, indicate the social disorder which has led to many forms of social deprivation of the indigenous peoples in an unequal society such as that of South Africa.

There is a subtle discrimination in treatment that is significant. The traditional possession that is good and desired is promoted by white medication. The *indiki* which is not so good is treated with red and white symbols, and *ufufunyane* which is thoroughly bad is treated with black and white medication. The grading of the evil spirit possessions signifies the intensity of the social malady which I suggest is represented by such evil possession.

There is yet another important difference between the traditional and new forms of spirit possession. In the case of the former relatively fewer people become diviners, and indeed diviners have to go through a long-drawn-out process, for possession of this type is gradual. In the case of the latter, possession is sudden, and may even assume the form of an epidemic in a given area. The epidemic nature and the element of sudden attack strongly point to the association of new forms of possession with stresses and strains that may be experienced by people as a group at a particular point in time. (This parallels the increasing cases of nervous breakdown at institutions of higher education before or during important examinations.)

It would be naive to imagine that the possessed consider themselves as expressing the above sociological notions. It is the philosophers of the society who have interpreted the manifestations of such deviant behaviour in such a way that it lends itself to sociological analysis. I refer to the diviners and doctors whose function it is to understand the various types of illness, explain the new ones and find relevant treatment.

What has emerged from this presentation is that there are various levels of spirit possession. On the one hand there is the traditional, morally acceptable spirit possession of the diviners (*izangoma*), and on

the other hand there is the evil, undesirable and unacceptable possession of the *ufufunyane* type. In addition, there are the "in between" forms
of possession, which may begin as evil and be developed to become
morally acceptable, i.e. of the *indiki* type.

There is yet another form of possession which I have not yet mentioned. This is the temporary possession experienced by the faithful
during worship in the Zionist or Pentecostal sects. It is not as continuous as in the other forms of possession discussed above. However, a
Prophet (or Prophetess) in such sects may be thought of as being in
continuous contact with the spirit. In that case his role is seen as more
or less identical with that of a diviner.

What I am saying is that it is important to distinguish between the
various levels of possession in order to understand the meaning of spirit
possession. For instance, the people possessed by the good spirits often
belong to the priestly class (diviners, prophets).

Whereas in some societies the "calling" to the position of priesthood
is reserved for men only, in others it is reserved for women. Looked at
in this light, such women (the diviners among the Zulu) are playing a
role that is set for them by the society for the benefit of the society. They
are not primarily looking for outlets in an unequal, male-dominated
society, as some anthropologists suggest, e.g. Gluckman (1955),
Hammond-Tooke (1962), Lee (1969).

In attaining the status of diviner, a candidate goes through various
phases of experience, such as abstinence from various pleasurable things
(e.g. drinks, smoking, sexual intercourse, certain foods), withdrawal
from society, observance of silence, avoidance of unclean situations (i.e.
contact with death), and engaging in ecstatic singing and dancing. All
such experiences are forms of asceticism calculated to achieve a desired
contact with the sacred realm, a practice found in many religions in
one way or another, as part of a "priestly" behaviour pattern.

Possession by alien spirits (*ufufunyane*) is diametrically opposed to
possession by ancestral spirits. It is this type of possession which can be
linked with psychogenic disorder, as indeed Loudon (1965, 1959), Lee
(1969) and Lewis (1971) point out. It seems to be an aftermath of
colonialism related to intrusions by alien peoples into Zulu culture.

I believe, however, that Lewis in his interpretation of this type of
possession overstresses its relationship to the weak and the deprived. He
sees it mainly as a means used by the weak to gain certain favours from
the strong, as in a wife/husband relationship where the spirit possessing

the wife may want a new dress or good food. Although this may be true up to a point, it is nevertheless not the central explanation of evil possession by alien spirits. I see the notions of alien spirit possession as closely related to the extreme form of depression or nervous breakdown which may be coupled with hysteria and suicidal tendencies.

Depression of this nature is not typical of South African peoples alone. But the manner of handling various forms of mental disturbance differs from society to society.

Zulu handle mentally disturbed people in such a way that they do not feel responsible for their condition; they are not made to feel that anything is wrong with their minds, but merely that they are victims of external forces—the intruding alien spirits—which must be removed. The patient gets the support, sympathy and attention that depressed people often long for.

Because *ufufunyane* patients even after recovery are believed to be still susceptible to *ufufunyane* attacks if provoked or annoyed, those around them must take special care to avoid situations that might make *ufufunyane* recur. Whisson (1964) reports the same notion among the Luo of East Africa, where the patient, although pronounced fit, is treated with respect and consideration lest the dreaded affliction recurs.

If we accept that spirit possessions of the *ufufunyane* type are symptoms of various forms of extreme depression or nervous breakdown, precautions taken become understandable, as people who have had such mental confusion become vulnerable in the face of stress and strain. They must take care and avoid situations of anxiety or strenuous mental exercise.

What I am suggesting here is that the notion of evil spirit possession is used among the Zulu as an idiom to handle the escalating proportions of psychoneurosis often associated with failure to cope with the changing way of life in the colonial and post-colonial industrial society.

The infants' ailments associated with evil spirit possession have an expressive significance if we consider that in both situations the terms used are those of food containers. *Igobongo* means a dried, deseeded gourd or calabash. When used to contain sour milk, *amasi*, the highly valued traditional Zulu staple diet, a gourd is referred to as *igula*; but if it is empty it is *igobongo*. *Igobongo* essentially means "emptiness". Indeed Doke and Vilakazi define the word as follows in their Dictionary: "Hollow place or thing, empty container as a calabash, hollow tree, hollow place beneath the ground, empty egg-shell."

Ipleti is used to refer to the mythical malformed placenta. The term
used for a normal placenta is *umzanyana*. (*Umzali*, parent; diminutive,
umzalinyana or, in shortened form, *umzanyana*. The term is also used for
a nurse girl who minds the baby while its mother attends to domestic
chores.) The placenta, as the Zulu sees it, is a "little parent", as its
function is to provide the baby in the womb with the necessities for its
growth. By contrast, the placenta in its supposedly malformed state is
referred to as "just a plate"—an empty plate. It seems to me that there
is more in the meanings of these infant ailments than meets the eye.
Both *igobongo* and *ipleti* are terms used in a manner that suggests deprivation and starvation.

Zulu practitioners in interpreting mental disturbances[1] such as
ufufunyane or *indiki* do not only recognize them as related to failure to
cope with the changing social life, but also realize how the new disruptive social forces could threaten the very existence and continuity
of Zulu society as a distinct entity. Hence prophylactic measures must
be taken at a mystical level of treatment to reassure the people that
their young are protected by the *ipleti* and *igobongo* treatment.

---

[1] Zulu distinguish between different levels of mental disorder. For instance, a schizophrenic
person is said to be mad (*uhlanya*) and not possessed by any spirits. An epileptic suffers from
isithuthwane, an incurable condition. He is not possessed by the spirits. Some people may
suffer from a form of hysteria (*umhayizo*) whereby they weep aloud uncontrollably and are
not necessarily possessed, if they do not show other symptoms of mental confusion.

9 | Conclusion

My main aim in this book has been to show that Zulu ideas and beliefs relating to illness and its treatment are part of a coherent body of knowledge that lends itself to being interpreted and analysed in a framework of sociological theory. Given this emphasis, I have had to limit myself to the essential ethnographic data, leaving out much detail.

I would also have liked to put the Zulu ideas into proper perspective within the Nguni group as a whole, and see to what extent what I have said for the Zulu applies to the other Nguni societies. In this I have been hampered by the insufficient literature in the field of health and disease.

To round off my study, I should like to underline a few points by briefly recapitulating the implications of the Zulu material regarding some current anthropological theories.

Because it is Professor Max Gluckman perhaps more than any other anthropologist who has used the Zulu ethnographic data to support some of his theoretical contributions to our understanding of social anthropology, my remarks in this chapter are concerned chiefly with his work. I am fully aware that some of the shortcomings in his analysis were due to the incomplete ethnographic data, and others could perhaps be attributed to his legal training, which put into prominence the legal aspects of social life, thus playing down the familial permutations. So my comments must be seen as more concerned with clarifying the issues by adding certain dimensions to those issues already raised by Gluckman.

I have already shown that the understanding of evil as a mystical entity which can be removed from the body system and discarded as a substance modifies various theories put forward on some aspects of Zulu rituals. I particularly have in mind Gluckman's theory about "The Rituals of Rebellion" (1938, 1962, 1963, 1965). He sees the central theme of the Zulu first fruit ceremony (*umkhosi wokweshwama*) as concerned with expressing "integrative" rebellion, for, though hatred of the king is expressed by his rival brothers in the "hate" songs, these songs of hate and pronouncement of rejection are directed at the incumbent of kingship, and not at the institution of kingship itself. The rituals, Gluckman argues, thus provide an outlet to express discontent without necessarily removing the incumbent or revolting against the institution of kingship. In this sense the rituals provide a catharsis and have the effect of reinforcing the society.

Although this theory has provoked a great deal of critical response, notably from Beidelman (1966) and Raum (1967), I believe not enough attention has been given to the central theme of the Zulu ceremony—namely, ridding the whole kingdom (i.e. the land, people and king) of the evil influences that had accumulated during the previous year, and casting the evil in scapegoat fashion on the black bull, which is then burnt to cinders. The good things for the new year are achieved by sacrificial animals and white symbols, including medicinal symbols. The song of "hate" (in Bryant, 1949, p. 517: *Bayamzonda, bazond'inkosi,*[1] They hate him, they hate the king), which Gluckman has used as an operative point in his analysis, can be best understood if we remind ourselves that during the phase of treatment with black medicines the patients are believed to be intensely polluted with a condition of *umnyama*, which is understood to be a mystical force that weakens them and makes them accident-prone, as well as disagreeable and repulsive. The "hate" song therefore underlies this condition of repugnance and unpopularity (*isidina*) in the person of the king, who as the embodiment of the nation is polluted with an intense form of *umnyama* while going through the ritual phases calculated to purge the *umnyama* from the kingdom. Seen in this context the hate song can be said to be an item of ritual behaviour that is without any emotive connotation regarding either the king's subjects or his rival monarchs.

[1] I have had an opportunity of watching the ceremony twice and listening to the song at the Mafunze Chiefdom near Pietermaritzburg. The song was sung by everybody and not only by the princes as Gluckman suggests.

Incidentally, it is interesting that the theme of cleansing in these ceremonies did not sufficiently strike Bryant, in spite of the fact that the theme is categorically and repetitively spelt out in the Zulu texts he quotes. For instance, he writes:

> The performance at an end, the king, attended by the doctors, marched to the kraal entrance just outside of which he hurled another gourd, representing now his bitterest foe, to the ground and trampled triumphantly upon the fragments, the while the encompassing army shouted "Wu! Wu! Wu!" and he himself shouted *"Wawa umswazi!"*, and so uMswazi (the Swazi king, and particular foe intended) fell! 1949, p. 520

Bryant here has completely mistranslated the Zulu term *umswazi*,[1] which he says means "the Swazi people", whereas in fact it means pollution and is a synonym of *umnyama*. What the king breaks to pieces and tramples upon is a gourd that symbolizes the evil of the past year. The seriousness of a translation error of this nature needs no emphasis, as it can be compounded by later writers using the erroneous information as source material. Translated correctly, Bryant's Zulu text gives yet another indication of the central position of a purging notion in the theme of Zulu first fruit ceremonies.

In a recent paper on the implications of women's fecundity Gluckman writes:

> A duty is laid on women married from outside into a group of agnates, that they bear sons to perpetuate their husband's groups. But the effect of the birth of sons is to produce competitors for the limited land, cattle and important positions and privileges of each group. . . . Since the conflict in pursuit of goals arises from the birth of sons it means that wives both strengthen and weaken the group when they discharge their duty to be fertile. This conflict arising from the duty laid on women is concealed by the belief that they are witches moved by insatiable sexual desires. . . .
>
> A man must deliberately make the choice to attack another, either openly by force or secretly by practising the evil magic of a sorcerer. Women are witches, with inherent evil power. . . . 1972, p. 14

I have argued that, contrary to Gluckman's assertion, women are not witches. They may be polluted from time to time, but they are

---

[1] Doke and Vilzkai, Zulu/English Dictionary:

sing. *umswazi*; pl. *imiswazi*
1. Bad luck, misfortune. 2. Bad odour, stench.
sing. = i(li) *Swazi*; pl. =amaSwaz.
1. Member of the Swazi tribe. 2. Assegai with grooved blade made in Swaziland.

certainly not regarded as witches. There is indeed no conventional concept of witchcraft among the Zulu, because a person who harms another always does so intentionally and has conscious control of his actions. This is conventionally regarded (by anthropologists) as sorcery rather than witchcraft.

I have further pointed out that, within the homestead married women, who are outsiders and often rivals, usually accuse each other of sorcery. This situation is aggravated and accentuated by the norm that only the agnates (and not the married women) within the homestead are enjoined by religious sanctions against sorcerizing one another. Such is the situation as it operates within the homestead. However, as soon as segmentation of the homestead takes place, the brothers who had hitherto been constrained by religious sanctions find themselves in a position to practise lineage sorcery against their agnatic kin without fear of ancestral intervention. The notion of lineage sorcery suggests a developmental cycle in sorcery accusation, where first a man's wives, and later on his grown-up sons as homestead heads, compete for the good things of life. Gluckman does not mention the significance of lineage sorcery in his analysis, but I believe it is very relevant and essential in analysing the structural frame within which sorcery operates.

I agree with him in regarding the position of married women within an extended homestead as the weak point in the unity of corporate agnatic groups, in that within such groups they form boundaries for smaller uterine units. It is this position of women that may be seen as a danger. However, I must stress that this danger is not viewed as an "evil inherent in women", as Gluckman suggests, because sorcery is not a prerogative of women only. In fact sorcery as practised by men is believed to be more devastating, in the sense that a man as a lineage sorcerer or as a night sorcerer (and a woman cannot be either) destroys other homestead heads and their dependants, crop and stock. While a man practises devastating sorcery, a woman's sorcery is often directed against one particular person she is in conflict with.

I see the stress laid by Gluckman on the mystical powers of women's fecundity as related more to notions of pollution than of witchcraft; a woman's fecundity gives rise to dangerous impurity not because she is evil-hearted but because she is a woman. It is of further interest that the Zulu, who do not place emphasis on witchcraft as an inherent evil, have elaborate notions of impurity in relation to women. There is a parallel here with many African societies which have notions of witchcraft, the inherent evil often associated with women, while sorcery, the conscious act, is associated with men.

Zulu women in their state of pollution endanger men, cattle and crops. In other words, while sorcery on a comprehensive scale can be regarded as a man's thing, pollution is essentially a woman's thing. The significant feature, however, in the opposition is that while a man is in control of his action as a sorcerer, a woman is not in control of the situations which make her impure. This is consistent with the notion that men have control of power and authority and women do not.

The notion of pollution further places an essential stress in the Zulu understanding of illness, namely that illness is mainly a woman's business. Her duties as a mother place her from time to time in a dangerous position—a danger to herself and to others. Her task is to safeguard herself and those around her. She must be vigilant, take care to contain her vulnerability to illness, and forestall harmful consequences of her situation. A moral duty of this nature does not only imply control of her movements in time and space but also emphasizes her identity as a distinct individual whose moral duty is to contribute to the welfare of the society, observing correct behaviour while undergoing experiences associated with reproduction to perpetuate the continuity of the society.

Apart from Gluckman's contributions, the Zulu system of ideas is of interest in regard to various present-day anthropological theories. For instance, the Levi-Straussian distinction of "The Raw and the Cooked" (1970) is reinforced by the Zulu notions of colour symbols in the treatment of disease, where black and red medicines are either decoctions or liquid placed in a red-hot potsherd in which the patients dip and then suck their fingers or medicinal substances burnt to produce smoke for inhalations. On the other hand white medicines are infusions and are never heated. In explaining this procedure Zulu said, *Imithi emnyama iyaphekwa, kanti emhlophe ayiphekwa, idliwa iluhlaza*, "black medicines are cooked, whereas white medicines are not cooked; they are eaten raw". I have already indicated that black (and red) medicines are perceived as removing evil elements from the body system, while white medicines restore good health. I have argued that since the evil in this context derives from a social situation such as that of sorcery, ancestral wrath or pollution, all of which happen to a person because he is a member of the society, it therefore makes sense that cooking, which renders food a cultural item, is used to dichotomize (a) those medicines which represent social situations and are seen as removing

evil elements from a man as a human being, and (b) those raw medicines which are used to restore good health and to underline the fact
that a man as a natural creature is not ill.

One may well ask whether people are aware of this sophisticated
explanation. It is difficult to measure the extent of understanding, particularly because the implications of cooking or not cooking did not
occur to me while doing fieldwork and I therefore did not inquire into
the matter. None the less, it may help if we note that very often an
adult when reprimanding a child may say, "You are raw; you will be
cooked soft today" (*Uluhlaza uzovuthwa namhlanje*).[1] The implication is
that by punishing the child, a sense of good social behaviour will be
hammered into its head.

This suggests that the metaphors of cooking to instil a sense of good
behaviour, and of rawness to express crudeness, fit in with my argument
above that there are medicines which are cooked to symbolize the notion
of culture and medicines which are uncooked to indicate the notion
of nature, as indeed Levi-Strauss stresses that "such symbols make sure
that a natural creature is cooked and socialized" (1970, p. 336).

The Zulu usage of colour symbols in medicine further adds weight to
Turner's interpretation of the Ndembu colour symbols (Turner, 1967).
I have suggested that the Zulu rule of rigid sequence in the usage of
colour in medicine makes explicit what is implicit among the Ndembu,
namely, that the red symbols particularly represent transition, transformation and rebirth, while black and white symbols mainly represent
death and life respectively. This understanding makes sense in
interpreting situations such as those that keep cropping up in African
archaeological findings. For instance, Leakey (1931), quoted by Turner
(1967, p. 87), discovered in East Africa skeletons freely sprinkled with
red ochre. If red is seen more as a colour of transformation and transition it follows that red ochre and red paint on corpses and graves lay
extra stress on the notion of process—that is, the transformation of
human life into spiritual life.

Red as a colour of transformation for the Zulu, and the insistence on
sequential usage of colours with red in the middle, brings into prominence the processual or cyclical notion rather than the antithetical

---

[1] Although I have used this expression myself and also heard other people using it, it had
never occurred to me to analyse its real meaning. For this reason I believe on the whole
people are not aware of the social implications of the "raw and the cooked". Probably a few
people such as diviners and elders may understand the implications.

oppositions between either black and white, or red and white, or black and red or hot and cold.

With regard to ideas of evil spirits, I have argued that the Zulu evidence does not support Lewis's observation (1971). Lewis argues that possession by capricious and evil spirits shows a special predilection for the weak and down-trodden, and that through such possession the lowly secure a measure of help and succour. As an instance of this he cites cases of wives whose husbands provided them with good clothes and good food because the evil spirits possessing them demanded these objects.

While Lewis's interpretation may apply to occasional instances, I find it difficult to accept as a central theme in explaining evil spirit possession, partly because it suggests malingering, which is difficult to gauge in a cultural context that regards the illness as genuine, and also because the effects of evil spirits are seen by the Zulu as a threat to the whole community. When, for instance, infants are believed to be in danger that necessitates elaborate and expensive prophylactic treatment (see *ipleti*; *igobongo*: Chapter 8) the infants thus protected against the potential ill effects of evil spirits can hardly be said to be malingering in the hope of getting special favours from their parents.

I have therefore suggested that since the notion of evil possession is a post-colonial concept,[1] it may well be that the unsettling conditions of the industrial era do give rise to certain stresses and strains. I find it significant that in the main the evil spirits are spirits of aliens—a point which indicates the sensitivity of the indigenous peoples to alien intrusions. Seen in this light evil spirits possession can be understood to be an idiom used to indicate various forms of mental disturbance arising from new demands in an industrial society.

With regard to the ancestral spirits, I have suggested that since the jurally effective ancestors are seen as consisting mainly of one's parents and one's father's parents, it follows that the power of the ancestors rests on this very shallowness of the ancestral depth. I have indicated how the ancestors are often said to interfere with the health of infants, thereby threatening to deprive those infants' parents of ancestral status when they later on reach the spirit world, as they would have no progeny to give them such status. The shallowness of ancestral depth thus enables the current ancestors to pressurize the living (who would

---

[1] One could postulate that this is due to the fact that before colonialism there had never been large-scale and protracted unsettling and disruptive influences.

in due course supersede them in the cycle of development) to conform to the norms and duties expected of them. This is a crucial point to understand in order to appreciate some aspects of the mechanics of relationship between the living and the dead.

In the interpretation of illness and its treatment, we see an elaborate and ordered system of ideas and practice. It is a coherent view that prevails even now in a society which has faced repeated and continued stresses. It probably has sustained the people and provided them with deep and satisfying answers to suffering brought by illness and misfortune.

Perhaps it is for this reason that it endures despite tremendous alteration in the material and social circumstances of present-day Zulu life.

Appendix 1

I have selected several texts to represent the type of information I gathered during fieldwork.

They represent what was reiterated by various informants, whose statements were never conflicting. They consequently reflect a consensus on basic features of ideology in relation to Zulu cosmology.

The problem with texts is that certain ideas that are unwritten but understood by the speakers of the language cannot come through in verbatim translation. Because of this I have in each case re-written the passages in a more conventional English style to convey such hidden ideas.

Owing to limitations of space I cannot present texts that cover adequately all the notions I have discussed.

What I have selected has some bearing on ideas about ancestral spirits, colour symbols in medicine, sorcery, pollution and the notions of symmetry in social relations.

Some ideas on ancestors[1]

BAGCINA BENZENJANI LABO APAFA KUDALA ABANGASABIZWA UMA KUHLATSHIWE?
(What ultimately happens to those who died long ago and are no longer mentioned when slaughtering?)

1. *Batshela   laba   ababaziyo   ukuthi ababaqoqe*
   They tell these they know that   they should gather together
   bonke.—Bayabazike   bona. Labo   abasenawo
   all.   They know them well, they. Those who still have
   amandla   okufika   ngolaka, — bafika   ngobuhle
   a right (or power) of coming with anger—they come with goodness

---

[1] Text from three different informants.

Kudliwa.   *Abanamandla*   *okufika   ngolaka*
in a festive situation.   Those who have a right of coming with anger
bagcina kobabamkhulu.
stop   at grandfather (generation of ancestors).
(The people who sacrifice) tell those (ancestors) they know that they should invite
all the ancestral spirits who should be invited. The ancestors know such spirits.
Those ancestors who still have the right or power to reward or punish come to
participate in the sacrificial meal and bring good fortunes to the descendants.
Ancestors who have such jural power are not beyond the grandfather generation.

2. *Esibizana   nabo   abozalo   lukababamkhulu*
The people we invite with are of birth of grandfather
Uzalo   lukababa   kababamkhulu asisabizani
Those of birth of the father of grandfather we no longer invite
nalo   ngoba   sesandıle   sesizele   nathi
with them because we have increased we have given birth also
sibaningi.
we are many.

   The people with whom we (mutually) have an obligation to invite on sacrificial
occasions are lineage members who are descendants of our grandfather. We no
longer have mutual religious obligations with lineage members descended from
our great grandfather. Because we have increased in number, there are too many
of us.

3. *U-Ma   ufika   ehamba   nabanakwabo   akade*
My mother comes accompanied (or going) with *abanakwabo* already
edla   nabo esaphila   —Akezi   nabakubo
she ate with while alive.   She does not come with her own people.
Kwabakubo—   uMa   uye   aye   kwabakubo
To her own people mother does go   to her own people
athi anongivakashela   emzini   wami
says "You should visit me at home mine
Kunomsebenzi. —   Kodwa   akadli   nabo
there is *umsebenzi.*   But she does not eat with them
sithebe   sinye.   Emhlabeni   kusaphilwa
from the tray one and the same.   In this world when people still alive
sibanika   indlu yabo njengabantu base
we give them house theirs as people   of an
mzini. —   Kukhishwe   isithebe   notshwala
affinal homestead.   It is brought out the tray and beer
kubekwe   kubona.
it is placed to them.

   When my mother as an ancestress comes home (when we sacrifice) she comes
with her "sisters in marriage", the spirits of the wives married into the lineage
segment, who were either her co-wives or wives of her husband's brothers who
reciprocally call each other *zakwethu* (*zakwabo*—third person speaking). These are
the women with whom she used to eat sacrificial meat from the same tray while
alive.

She never returns as an ancestress (of her descendants) in the company of her own people's ancestral spirits. In the spirit world, she invites her own people's spirits to come to the sacrifice as guests. But, when the spirits of her own people come as visitors in this way my mother's spirit does not eat with them.

During her lifetime when my mother's people were invited on the occasion of *umsebenzi*, we placed them in a separate house (hut) as special guests as they were affinal people (*abantu basemzini*). We gave them meat on a special tray (*isithebe*) and beer in a special pot.

Note (a) The emphasis here on the mother coming with her sisters in marriage does not mean that women come home as spirits on such festive occasions without the company of their husbands. It merely means that she is the hostess to her sisters in marriage as she used to be during her lifetime, while her husband was a host to his brothers. The passage also emphasizes the importance of motherhood in the context of the spirit world.

(b) *Umsebenzi* is a term which in everyday usage means a job, work, or occupation. When used in the ritual context it means a sacrifice usually on a large scale, which involves the killing of goats and oxen. It is, however, used also for lesser sacrifices in its comprehensive sense which covers all types of sacrifices. Each sacrifice, however, has a particular name which usually indicates the intention of the sacrifice.

(c) *Umuzi* is a term which means "a homestead". But if used in the context of *abantu basemzini*, it means affines.

Ideas on colour symbolism and sorcery

Umuthi   omnyama   unezinto   ozizilelayo   njengenyama
The medicine which is black has its things which you avoid such as meat
namafutha.   Awudli   nomuntu
and fat.   You do not eat (from the same dish) with another person.
awuyi   endodeni.   Uziqoqe   uzile   uxwaye
You do not go to a man.   You restrain yourself abstain avoid
nezinkomo   namasimu   namasi.
even the cattle and the fields and curdled milk.
Umuthi   obomvu   ukhipha   omnyama.
The medicine which is red pushes out the black.
Usuke   kobomvu   ufune   omhlophe.
You set off from the red you look for the white.
Omhlophe   ukhipha   obomvu.
The white pushes out the red.
Uma   usudla   obomvu   usuphakathi
When you eat the red you are now in the between
nendawo.   Usazila   kancane
space.   You still abstain a little
ufishi namafutha awuwadli,   kodwa ayi kakhulu njenga   udla
fish   and fat   you do not eat, but   not as much as when you eat

imithi emnyama.   *Omhlophe   ukhipha   obomvu,*
medicines which are black.   The white pushes out the red.
usukhululekile.   *Usuthandwa   na-abantu.*
You are now released.   You are now liked even by people.
Isidina   *ukhipha   umnyama   nje*
In a condition of "disagreeableness" you take out the pollution merely
esingajulile   njengomnyama.
it is not of a deep dimension as the usual pollution (*umnyama*).

While treated with black medicines, one avoids certain things such as eating meat or fat or eating together with people who are not themselves being treated with black medicines. One abstains from sexual intercourse, restrains one's behaviour in general, i.e. withdraw from gatherings, avoid contact with cattle, with crops and with milk.

The red medicines supersede the black medicines and the white medicines supersede the red medicines.

During the treatment with red medicine one is "in between". The rules of abstention and avoidance observed during the period of black medical treatment become much more relaxed when one takes red medicines. One, however, still abstains from eating such things as fish and fat.

When one takes white medicines after red medicines one is released from all restrictions and abstentions. One mixes with people and exchanges pleasantries ("You are now liked even by people").

Conditions of pollution are of different intensity. For instance the condition of "disagreeableness" known as *isidina* is a condition of pollution which is not of high intensity ("deep dimension") as the other forms of pollution (such as that associated with birth and death).

Emva kokudla amakhubalo   abomvu   kusa
After eating the strong medicines which are red on the following morning
uphalaze   nge "dulla"   elimhlophe.   Umithi   omnyama
you vomit with the *dlula* which is white.   The medicines which are black
ukhipha   umnyama   nobomvu   ubalelwa   izinsuku
you take out the pollution even the red one also you count the days
uwudla   bese   ukhishwa.
of eating it and then it is taken out or pushed out.
Ayidliwa   ingakhishwa.
They are never eaten and not taken out again or pushed out.

In cases of bereavement (*-amakhubalo abomvu* are red medicines reserved for treating the bereaved) people are treated with red medicines and this is followed up by white emetic treatment on the following day.

Neither black nor red medicines are retained: they must be expelled and super-seded by white medicines.

Abantu besifazane   bavama ukuxabana ikakhulu   esithenjini
People of female sex usually quarrel   more particularly in polygynous marriage
baze   bathakathelane.   Amadoda wona athakatha nje
they eventually sorcerize one another.   The men them sorcerize merely

ngoba   esuke   evele   ewumthakathi   ngenhliziyo.
because right from the start being inclined being a sorcerer with his heart.
Abe   nomona afise   umthakathi we ndoda   uvama
He becomes jealous and covetous, a sorcerer of male sex usually (inclined)
ukubulala amanye amadoda nako   konke   okwayo.   Kanti
to kill   other   males   and all everything that is theirs,   whereas
isifazane   siqonda   lowo.   Kuke
the female aim straight at a particular one (person).   It sometimes
kwenze   ingane ibulale   uyise   ikakhulu
happens (that) a child kills (or sorcerizes) the father more particularly
inkosana ifuna   ifa.   Kodwa   ayi   unina.
an heir wanting the inheritance.   However, not (or never) the mother.
Kanti   naye   uyise   uyayibulala   inkosana.
After all he also the father is capable of killing (sorcerizing) the heir.
Kodwa-Ke   akuvamile   neze.
However indeed, it is not common at all.

Women usually quarrel. This happens more particularly in a polygynous situation and their quarrel may even lead to sorcery practice. Men who are sorcerers are usually "evil-hearted" by nature. They are jealous and covetous. Such male sorcerers usually practice sorcery against other men who are also homestead heads. Their sorcery is much more devastating in that it does not only affect the victim but everything that belongs to him (i.e. the dependants, cattle, and crops). A woman sorcerer on the other hand harms the particular person she is in conflict with.

Occasionally it does happen that a son who is an heir practises sorcery against his father in order to gain inheritance. A son hardly ever practises sorcery against his mother. On the other hand a father may practise sorcery against the heir. However, sorcery between father and son is very rare.[1,2]

Ideas on pollution and balance[3]

SHONO UKUTHI NTOZINI (a) EZIZILWA (b) EZIGCINIVA
(Explain what is (a) avoided, (b) observed)
        (c) SHONO UKUTHI UKUPHULA IMITHETHO
        (What the result of the breach is)
        (d) INGALUNGISWA KANJANI?
        (How can it be put right?)
        (e) ZIKHOMNA IZENZO EZENZIWAYO UKUZE UMPHUMELA
        WOKUNGAZILI UPHANGALALE?
        (Is there a ritual which forestalls the
        results of the breach?)

[1] The informant is emphasizing here that although such sorcery is not expected, it is possible. In other words she is saying that people do break the rules—people "sin" sometimes.
[2] The informant was a diviner.
[3] The informant was a diviner. But she was not the diviner who gave information on colour symbolism and sorcery.

1. UMUNTU WESIFAZANE OSESIKHATHINI

(A menstruating woman)

Akawadli   amasi.   Esibabeni   akayi   uma
She does not eat milk curd.   To the cattle byre she does not go when
ziwu 8   izinsuku asinde.   Uya ya   nje
they are 8 the days she smears the floor. Although she does go
emsindweni   kodwa axwaye   isilisa,   nabagulayo
to gatherings but   she avoids the male sex, and the sick
nemithi   yabo akasondeli   kuyona ngoba
and the medicines theirs she does not come close to them because
usuke   emi   kabi.
simply of being standing badly[1] (i.e. not in good order).

A menstruating woman abstains from eating milk food. She keeps away from the cattle byre. After eight days she cleans the floor of the hut she lives in by smearing it with cow dung. Although she may go to gatherings, she must avoid mixing with men. She also keeps away from the sick and their medicines because in her condition of disorder or lack of balance ("standing badly") she may be a danger to the sick and their medicine.

2. OWESIFAZANE OSANDA KUZALA

(A mother who has newly delivered a baby and is still bleeding)

Uhlala   yedwa aze   aqede   8 days edla   yedwa.
She lives alone until she finishes 8 days eating alone.
Asinde   aphume.   Angayi
She then smears the floor, and then goes out. She does not go to
emsindweni. Ugcoba   ibomvu   kuze kuphele
gatherings. She smears herself with red ochre until it is finished
izinyanga   ezintathu   bese   egeza
the months (or moons) which are three and then she washes off
ibomvu.   Phela   unjengomuntu   ofelwe
the red ochre.   Indeed you are like a person who is bereaved
uma uzele.   A   Kuvunyiwe   ukuthi kungene umuntu
if   you have given birth.   (It is not allowed that   enters   a person
wesilisa.
of male sex.)

A newly delivered mother withdraws from the society for eight days during which time she eats alone. After eight days she cleans the house (hut) in which she is confined by smearing the floors with cow dung. She may then come out of total confinement, but still does not go to gatherings. For three months she has her body smeared with red ochre. After three months she stops covering her body with red ochre. Indeed a mother in her post-partum stage is like a person who is bereaved (i.e. a chief mourner). Men are not allowed to enter the house while she is still confined.

---

[1] I think the expression "standing badly" here portrays the notion of imbalance very well.

3. UMUNTU OSHONEKWE
   (A bereaved person)
   Uhlala phansi angaphekeli   *abantu*   *aqede*   *amasonto*
   She sits down, she does not cook for people, she finishes weeks
   amabili a pheke   *adle*   *yedwa ngesipunu*   *sakhe*
   two being cooking, being eating alone with a spoon of hers,
   angakhulumi   *nabantu.*   *Nabazombona*
   she does not speak with people.   Even those who come to condole with
   akakhulumi.   *Kukhuluma*   *abanye athule*   *nje*   *yena.*
   her, she does not speak.   It is speaking others keeps quiet merely—she.

   The chief mourner withdraws from society and is confined to the house. Other people do not eat what she has cooked; she alone eats it and she uses her own special eating utensils. She is secluded in this fashion for two weeks after bereavement, during which time she does not speak to people. Even those who come to offer their condolences speak to other women who keep the bereaved company.

4. OBULELE OMUNYE
   (A homicide)
   Uyaphalaza akhiphe   *iqungo.*   *Uyazila*   *ahlale*
   He vomits to take out blood-lust. He abstains, he stays
   endlini   *njengomuntu*   *ofelwe.*   *Angayi*
   in the house like a person who is bereaved. He does not
   nakowesifazane.
   go to a person of female sex.

   The homicide is treated with emetic medicines to remove the condition of blood-lust. He withdraws from society, is confined to the house like a person who is bereaved (i.e. a chief mourner). He abstains from sexual intercourse.

5. YIBHUNGU ELISHAYWE YIZIBUKO
   (A young man who has experienced nocturnal emission)
   Uvuka   *kungakasi*   *ayogeza*   (*Akasazikhiphi izinkomo*).
   He gets up before dawn and go to bathe. (He no longer takes out cattle).
   Abuye   *adle*   *isiqunga.*   *Uya*   *njalo nje*
   He returns and he eats *isiqunga* medicine. He goes always
   emfulemi   *uma limshayile*   *aze*   *ashade*
   to the river if experienced nocturnal emission until he marries
   noma aze   *aqonywe.*
   or until he has a girl.

   A youth who has had involuntary nocturnal emissions (*ukushaywa izibuko*) gets up before dawn to bathe in the river. On his return he treats himself with *isiqunga* which belongs to the white class of medicines. He behaves in this way every time he has an involuntary nocturnal emission until he marries or until he has a girl friend with whom he has sex and emits in sexual intercourse.[1]

---

[1] What is noteworthy in the above texts is that there are consistent parallels made by the informant. She points out that the newly delivered mother is like a chief mourner and also points out that the homicide is like a chief mourner. This conforms to the parallels I have presented in connection with pollution.

Appendix 2

Glossary

Since I have translated Zulu words when using them, I list here only those that appear frequently in the text.

-bomvu	Red
ukudlisa	To poison; to add harmful substances to food
ufufunyane	Evil possession by thousands of spirits of alien societies
umhlahlo	A public consultation with a diviner by protagonists
umkhondo	A dangerous track of wild animals or people
umkhuhlane	General appellation for all natural illnesses such as fevers and colds
-luhlaza	Green or blue; raw
umeqo	Illness arising from stepping over a harmful concoction
-mhlophe	White
-mnyama	Black; dark
umndeni	Lineage
indiki	Evil possession by male spirits of African origin, but not of the same patrilineage as the medium
isangoma	Diviner, Shaman
umnumzane	Homestead head
umnyama	Darkness, pollution, impurity, misfortune, poor luck
inyanga	A male doctor practising Zulu medicine
umuthi	Medicine (tree)
uzalo	Lineage
ukuzila	Abstinence
umuzi	Homestead

Bibliography

Beidelman, T. O. (1966). Swazi royal rituals. *Africa*, 373–404.

Berlin, B. and Kay, P. (1969). "Basic Colour Terms". University of California Press, Berkeley and Los Angeles.

Bryant, A. T. (1929). "Olden Times in Zululand". Longmans, London.

Bryant, A. T. (1949). "The Zulu People". Shuter & Shooter, Pietermaritzburg.

Bryant, A. T. (1970). "Zulu Medicine and Medicine-Men". C. Struik, Cape Town.

Callaway, H. (1884). "The Religious Systems of the AmaZulu". Publication of the Folk-Lore Society (XV).

Doke, C. M. and Vilakazi, B. W. (1953). "Zulu–English Dictionary". Witwatersrand University Press, Johannesburg.

Douglas, M. (1966). "Purity and Danger". Routledge & Kegan Paul, London.

Evans-Pritchard, E. E. (1937). "Witchcraft, Oracles and Magic among the Azande". Clarendon Press, Oxford.

Firth, R., Hubert, J. and Forge, A. (1970). "Families and their Relatives". Routledge & Kegan Paul, London.

Fortes, M. (1945). "The Dynamics of Clanship among the Tallensi". Oxford University Press, London.

Fortes, M. (1949). "The Web of Kinship among the Tallensi". Oxford University Press, London.

Fortes, M. (1959). "Oedipus and Job in West African Religion". University Press Cambridge.

Fortes, M. (1965). Some reflections on ancestor worship. *In* "African Systems of Thought" (Eds M. Fortes and G. Dieterlen). Oxford University Press, London.

Fortes, M. (1970). "Time and Social Structure". The Athlone Press, University of London, London.

Gluckman, M. (1938). Social aspects of first fruit ceremony among the South Eastern Bantu. *Africa*, **11**, 25–41.

Gluckman, M. (1963). "Custom and Conflict in Africa". Blackwell, Oxford.

Gluckman, M. (1963). "Order and Rebellion in Tribal Africa". Cohen & West, London.

Gluckman, M. (1965). "Politics, Law and Ritual in Tribal Society". Blackwell, Oxford.

Gluckman, M. (1972). Moral crises: magical and secular solutions. In "The Allocation of Responsibility" (Ed. M. Gluckman). University Press, Manchester.

Goody, J. (1956). "The Social Organization of the LoWiili". H.M. Stationery Office, London.

Goody, J. (1957). Fields of social control among the LoDagaba. *Journal of the Royal Anthropological Institute*, **87**, 75–104.

Goody, J. (1959). The mother's brother and the sister's son in West Africa. *Journal of the Royal Anthropological Institute*, **89**, 61–88.

Goody, J. (1962). "Death, Property and the Ancestors". Tavistock Publications, London.

Hammond-Tooke, W. D. (1970). Urbanization and interpretation of misfortune: a quantitative analysis. *Africa*, **40**, 25–39.

Hammond-Tooke, W. D. (1962). "Bhaca Society". Oxford University Press, Cape Town.

Hunter, M. (1961). "Reaction to Conquest". (2nd edition.) Oxford University Press for the International African Institute.

Hyman, H. L. (1922). "Comparative Vertebrate Anatomy". University of Chicago Press, Chicago.

James, W. (1902). "The Varieties of Religious Experience". Longmans Green, London. Republished (1960) by Fontana, London.

Junod, H. A. (1913). "The Life of a South African Tribe", vol. II. Imprimerie Attinger Press, Neuchatel.

Krige, E. J. (1950). "The Social System of the Zulus". Shuter & Shooter, Pietermaritzburg.

Krige, E. J. (1968). Girls' puberty songs and their relation to fertility, health, morality and religion among the Zulu. *Africa*, **38**, 173–198.

Kohler, M. (1941). "The Izangoma Diviners". Ethnological publication 9. Department of Native Affairs, Pretoria.

Laubscher, B. J. F. (1937). "Sex, Custom and Psychopathology". Routledge & Kegan Paul, London.

Leach, E. (1964). Anthropological aspects of language animal categories and verbal abuse. In "New Directions in the Study of Language" (Ed. E. H. Lenneberg). M.I.T. Press, Cambridge, Massachusetts.

Leach, E. (1965). The nature of war. *Disarmament and Arms Control*, **3**, 165–183.

Leach, E. (1970). "Levi-Strauss". Fontana/Collins.

Leach, E. (1971). Kimil—a category of andamanese thought. In "Structural Analysis of Oral Traditions" (Eds P. and E. K. Maranda). University Press, Pennsylvania.

Leakey, L. S. B. (1931). "The Stone Age Cultures of Kenya Colony". Oxford University Press, London.

Lee, S. G. (1950). Some Zulu concepts of psychogenic disorder. *Journal of Social Science*.

Lee, S. G. (1969). Spirit possession among the Zulu. (Eds J. Beattie and J. Middleton.) In "Spirit Mediumship and Society in Africa". Routledge & Kegan Paul, London.

Levi-Strauss, C. (1970). "The Raw and the Cooked" (English translation). Jonathan Cape, London.

Lewis, I. M. (1971). "Ecstatic Religion". Penguin Books, Harmandsworth.

London, J. B. (1959). Psychogenic disorder and social conflict among the Zulu (Ed. M. K. Opler). In "Culture and Mental Health". Macmillan, New York.

London, J. B. (1965). Social aspects of ideas about treatment (Eds A. V. S. van Reuch and R. Porter). In "Ciba Foundation Symposium on Transcultural Psychiatry". J. and A. Churchill, London.

Marwick, B. A. (1966). "The Swazi". Nelson, London and Edinburgh.

Mbatha, M. B. (1960). Migrant labour and its effects on tribal and family life among the Nyuswa of Botha's Hill. Unpublished Master's thesis presented at the University of Natal.

McKnight, J. D. (1967). Extra-Descent Group Ancestor Cults in African Societies. *Africa*, **37**, 1–20.

Middleton, J. (1960). "Lugbara Religion: Ritual and Authority among an East African People". Oxford University Press for International African Institute, London.

Morris, D. R. (1966). "The Washing of the Spears". Oxford University Press, London.

Nyembezi, S. and Nxulamo, D. E. H. (1966). "Inqolobane Yesizwe". Shuter & Shooter, Pietermaritzburg.

Park, G. K. (1967). Divination in its social contexts. In "Magic Witchcraft and Curing" (Ed. J. Middleton). The Natural History Press, New York.

Peters, E. L. (1972). Aspects of the control of moral ambiguities: a comparative analysis of two culturally disparate modes of social control. In "The Allocation of Responsibility" (Ed. M. Gluckman). Manchester University Press, Manchester.

Radcliffe-Brown, A. R. (1952). "Structure and Function in Primitive Society". Routledge & Kegan Paul, London.

Raum, O. F. (1967). The Interpretation of the Nguni first fruit ceremony. *Paideuma*. Band XIII, pp. 148–163.

Reader, D. H. (1966). "Zulu Tribe in Transition". Manchester University Press, Manchester.

Sundkler, B. (1961). "Bantu Prophets in South Africa". Oxford University Press, London.

Turner, V. W. (1967). "The Forest of Symbols". Cornell University Press, New York.

Van Gennep, A. (1960). "The Rites of Passage". Routledge & Kegan Paul, London.

Vilakazi, A. (1962). "Zulu Transformation". University of Natal Press, Pietermaritzburg.

Whisson, M. G. (1964). Some aspects of functional disorders among the Kenya Luo (Ed. A. Kiev). In "Magic, Faith and Healing". Free Press, London.

Wilson, M. (1957). "Rituals of Kinship Among the Nyakyusa". Oxford University Press, London.

Subject Index

Name Index